THE

HISTORY AND ANTIQUITIES

OF THE CITY OF

ST. AUGUSTINE, FLORIDA.

THE

HISTORY AND ANTIQUITIES

OF THE CITY OF

ST. AUGUSTINE, FLORIDA

BY

GEORGE R. FAIRBANKS,

VICE-PRESIDENT OF THE FLORIDA HISTORICAL SOCIETY.

A FACSIMILE REPRODUCTION
OF THE 1858 EDITION,

WITH AN

INTRODUCTION and INDEX

BY

MICHAEL V. GANNON.

BICENTENNIAL FLORIDIANA
FACSIMILE SERIES.

A UNIVERSITY OF FLORIDA BOOK.

THE UNIVERSITY PRESSES OF FLORIDA.
Gainesville 1975.

BICENTENNIAL FLORIDIANA
FACSIMILE SERIES,
published under the sponsorship of the
BICENTENNIAL COMMISSION OF FLORIDA,
SAMUEL PROCTOR, *General Editor.*

A
FACSIMILE REPRODUCTION
OF THE 1858 EDITION,
WITH PREFATORY MATERIAL, INTRODUCTION,
AND INDEX ADDED.

Library of Congress Cataloging in Publication Data

Fairbanks, George Rainsford, 1820–1906.
　　The history and antiquities of the city of St.
Augustine, Florida.

　　(Bicentennial Floridiana Facsimile series)
　　Photoreprint of the ed. published by C. B. Norton,
New York.
　　"A University of Florida book."
　　Includes bibliographical references.
　　1. St. Augustine—History. 2. Florida—History
—To 1821. I. Title. II. Series.
[F319.S2F2　1975]　　　975.9′18　　　75–15750
ISBN 0–8130–0403–9

BICENTENNIAL
COMMISSION
OF FLORIDA.

Governor Reubin O'D. Askew, *Honorary Chairman*
Lieutenant Governor J. H. Williams, *Chairman*
Harold W. Stayman, Jr., *Vice Chairman*
Don Pride, *Executive Director*

Dick J. Batchelor, Orlando
Johnnie Ruth Clarke, St. Petersburg
A. H. Craig, St. Augustine
James J. Gardener, Fort Lauderdale
Jim Glisson, Tavares
Mattox Hair, Jacksonville
Thomas L. Hazouri, Jacksonville
Ney C. Landrum, Tallahassee
Mrs. Raymond Mason, Jacksonville
Carl C. Mertins, Pensacola
Charles E. Perry, Miami
W. E. Potter, Orlando
F. Blair Reeves, Gainesville
Richard R. Renick, Coral Gables
Jane W. Robinson, Cocoa

Mrs. Robert L. Shevin, Tallahassee
Don Shoemaker, Miami
Mary L. Singleton, Jacksonville
Bruce A. Smathers, Tallahassee
Alan Trask, Fort Meade
Edward Trombetta, Tallahassee
Ralph D. Turlington, Tallahassee
Robert Williams, Tallahassee
Lori Wilson, Merritt Island

GENERAL EDITOR'S PREFACE.

FLORIDA'S pre-eminent nineteenth-century historian was George Rainsford Fairbanks. Born and educated in the North, he moved south to St. Augustine to accept a judicial appointment in the territorial government of Florida. For the next sixty-four years of his life, Florida was his home. Most of this time he lived in St. Augustine, the oldest continuous settlement in what is now the United States. He was always intrigued with its rich and varied history and by the variety of people who made St. Augustine their home. In one of his first letters back to his family in New York, he noted that St. Augustine was "in all respects unlike any American town . . . its variety of inhabitants and mixture of languages gave it a peculiarly interesting character." Florida's colorful and romantic past excited him, and this was particularly true of St. Augustine. "About the old city," he wrote, "there clings a host of historic associations, which throw around it a charm which few can fail to feel." One of the great contributions to the heritage of this state is his history of St. Augustine, the first attempt to chronicle its story in the English language.

Fairbanks numbered among his Florida friends some of its most prestigious citizens, including Territorial Governor William P. DuVal, Moses Elias Levy and his son David, Florida's first United States senator, Kingsley Beatty Gibbs, who inherited the great Fort George Island plantation from his uncle, Zephaniah Kingsley, and Thomas Buckingham Smith, the diplomat and Spanish-Florida historian. While practicing law in St. Augustine, Smith had developed an interest in historical research, particularly in the area of the Spanish exploration and settlement. Perhaps it was his enthusiasm that influenced George Fairbanks to pursue similar studies of Florida's past.

Fairbanks first developed his interest in Florida history during the early 1850s. His reputation as a researcher and scholar quickly spread, and writers like Theodore Irving wrote seeking information on Spanish explorations in Florida. Fairbanks mastered the Spanish language so that he could read the history in the language of the original adventurers.

Early in 1856, Fairbanks and a group of his friends organized the Historical Society of Florida, the forerunner of the Florida Historical Society.

Many of the outstanding men in Florida politics joined the organization. At one of its first quarterly meetings, Fairbanks delivered a lecture to the society. "The Early History of Florida," as he titled the essay, was a survey of exploration and settlement from the time of Ponce de León to the English settlements in Georgia and the Carolinas in the seventeenth and eighteenth centuries. While Fairbanks' lecture was somewhat uneven and contained historical inaccuracies, it had both style and historic insight. It was so well-received that Fairbanks committed himself to write a book about St. Augustine. The remarkable result of this endeavor was *The History and Antiquities of the City of St. Augustine, Florida.*

Fairbanks was the first Florida historian to make major use of Spanish records in writing a serious historical account of St. Augustine's past. In addition, Fairbanks used extensively the writings of Barcia, Gonzalo Solís de Merás, Jacques le Moyne, Laudonnière, Gourgues, Carroll, Rivers, Simms, Roberts, Bartram, Stork, Romans, De Brahm, John Lee Williams, and William Cullen Bryant. *History and Antiquities* had great value for its time; without question it was the best summary of St. Augustine written to that date. The book was and is widely read and widely circulated. Every thorough bibliography of Florida history must include Fairbanks' study. It went through three editions, the first of which is reproduced here as a facsimile. It deserves its honored place in the annals of Florida historical scholarship.

George Fairbanks' reputation as a historian, researcher, and writer continues to be recognized to the present. He dedicated himself to exploring Florida's past and to keeping and preserving all that he discovered in trust for scholars and researchers who would follow him. This too is the theme for Florida's heritage program as it plans for its role in the nation's bicentennial.

The publication of facsimile editions of twenty-five rare, out-of-print volumes covering all periods of Florida's history, a series of pamphlets and monographs, the marking of a heritage trail, archaeological excavations, and historical restoration and preservation are major programs that are being sponsored by the Florida Bicentennial Commission. Each of the facsimile volumes includes an introduction written by a well-known authority in Florida history. These books, published for the Bicentennial Commission by the University Presses of Florida, Gainesville, are available at moderate prices to libraries, scholars, researchers, and all those interested in Florida's rich and colorful past.

The Florida Bicentennial Commission, a twenty-seven member agency, was created by the legislature to plan and develop Florida's role in the national bicentennial. Governor Reubin O'D. Askew

serves as honorary chairman of the commission.
Members of the legislature, the heads of state
agencies, and ten public members appointed by
the governor constitute the commission. Executive
offices are in Tallahassee.

Michael V. Gannon, professor of history and religion at the University of Florida, is the editor of
the facsimile of *The History and Antiquities of the
City of St. Augustine.* A former Basselin scholar
at the Catholic University of America, Dr. Gannon
received his bachelor and master degrees there in
philosophy. He is a graduate of the University of
Louvain in Belgium, and received his doctorate
degree in history at the University of Florida. His
books include *Rebel Bishop: The Life and Era of
Augustin Verot* and *The Cross in the Sand: The
Early Catholic Church in Florida, 1513-1870.* His
articles on the early Spanish period in Florida
have appeared in scholarly and professional
journals in the United States and Europe. In 1966
he received the Arthur W. Thompson Memorial
Prize in Florida History. from the Florida Historical Society for the best article published that year
in the *Florida Historical Quarterly.* Dr. Gannon is
a member of the Historic St. Augustine Preservation Board of the State of Florida. The government of Spain in 1974 awarded him the Knight
Cross of the Order of Isabella in recognition of his
research and publications in the field of Spanish-

Florida history. He is presently engaged in compil-
ing a documentary history of Florida, covering the
years to 1821.

SAMUEL PROCTOR

General Editor of the

BICENTENNIAL FLORIDIANA

University of Florida   FACSIMILE SERIES

INTRODUCTION.

St. Augustine is the oldest continuous settlement of European origin in what is now the United States of America. Founded September 8, 1565, forty years before Jamestown and fifty-five years before the Pilgrims landed at Plymouth Rock, it is the birthplace of western civilization and of Christianity in this country. Spaniards were the first to show the sails of their ships off its shoreline and the first, under Pedro Menéndez de Avilés, to put down roots and stay. But other peoples have contested for the city, and no less than four flags, at various times, have flown over its battlements, its narrow streets, and its balconied houses in the more than four centuries that it has stood. The rich and varied story of St. Augustine has been told many times, but the first attempt to do so in the English language is the present work, published here in facsimile, written in 1858 by George Rainsford Fairbanks. A resident of St. Augustine at the time, Fairbanks was the first Florida historian to make major use of Spanish records, and the first to essay a serious historical study of the city's past. Despite its faults, obvious to later historians with the advantage of a century's advance in discovery of sources and in development of the historiographic art, *The History and Antiquities of the City of St. Augustine, Florida* is a remarkable accomplishment for its time. In examining the life of its author, his times, his friends, and his historical sources, we learn how this book came to be and what place it deserves to hold in the annals of Florida historical scholarship.[1]

George Rainsford Fairbanks was born in Watertown, New York, July 5, 1820, one of four sons born to Jason and Mary Massey Fairbanks.[2] His father, a native of Mendon, Massachusetts, was in the saddle and harness business. Watertown was then a small mill village that drew power from the rapid fall of the Black River. Young George attended public school until eight or nine years of age, when he was transferred by his parents to a private school in the village run by a Mr. William Ruger, and at ten years of age he was sent on to Belville Academy in the countryside south of the village.

Fairbanks' father had commercial contacts in Montreal, Canada, and had acquired a taste for the French language and culture. Desiring that George and his older brother, Samuel, acquire the

same tastes, their father sent them to the Roman
Catholic Petit Séminaire at Montreal, a minor
seminary that prepared young men for the priest-
hood. George's father had no intention that his
two boys become Catholic priests—the family was
Protestant Episcopal—but he did want them to
have the advantage of the fine education for which
the seminary was renowned. George himself remembered in later life how difficult it was passing
from English to French, but after about five or six
months he found himself in possession of a considerable French vocabulary and at ease in both
formal class recitation and conversations with
schoolmates. Once a month he had leave to go outside the school, and he took advantage of those
times to eat dinner and speak English with friends
at an American hotel.

The meals at the seminary were healthy but
unimaginative. Lunch at noon consisted of one
large piece of bread, and at dinner there was meat,
bread, and vegetables. For about half the length
of each meal, eaten in common with all the other
students and professors, a student read a homily
from a high reading desk set against the wall of
the refectory. At the end of the reading, permission was given for talk, and a burst of voices would
sound forth. The students slept in dormitories,
long rooms each containing some thirty beds. As
at the meals, one of the boys was appointed to

read at night from a history tome, and thus the boys were lulled to sleep—not an experience, one presumes, to which one might attribute George's later interest in history. He remembered: "An old Scotch priest slept in a room adjoining and had an eye hole in his door so that he could, at any time, see the whole room and we never knew when that eye was at the eye hole. Sometimes he would come in, and if he found any boy uncovered, give him a smart slap as a reminder to cover himself."[3] George remained at the Petit Séminaire until July 1832, when a cholera epidemic forced his return to Watertown. Seventy-five to one hundred deaths were occurring daily, and the boys, when they went out, held small camphor bags under their noses as protection, so it was thought, against the disease. Like the other boys, George gave passersby a wide berth. Eventually, school was suspended, and the boys were sent back to their homes.

At Watertown, George was entered in a newly established academy built by public subscription and under the charge of a Presbyterian clergyman. Samuel entered Union College at Schenectady in 1835, and in September of the following year, at sixteen years of age, George entered the same institution. He was at the time, so he described himself, "a slight, slender, grey-eyed, ambitious boy."[4] With some two hundred other students he pursued studies in Latin, Greek, mathematics, chemistry, and moral philosophy. He had entered college as a sophomore but was much younger than the larger portion of his class. Nonetheless, he held a consistently high place on the class list. For a time he studied Hebrew and medicine, though his preference was for the classics, and in those disciplines he achieved his highest grades. His health was not good in those years, and he suffered severely from headaches in the fall of 1838, which required that he return to his home and absent himself from studies for a time. During that interval he worked in his father's store and achieved valuable business experience which would serve him well in later life.

Fairbanks graduated from Union College in 1839 and decided to prepare for the legal profession. To that end he read law in the office of W. A. Shumway, Esquire, a good lawyer of intemperate habits. George described him as "a man of fine parts but unfortunately at that time indulging in periodical sprees of a quiet, but absorbing character."[5] After a few months George transferred to the law office of Joseph Mullin, a young Irishman whom he much admired. Mullin would later be appointed to the Supreme Court of the State of New York. George was a diligent student, and in the spring of 1842 he was admitted to the bar of New York following a successful examination. He hung up his shingle, bearing gilt letters, at the foot of the staircase leading to Mr. Mullin's office.

Meantime, he had joined the New York state militia and had risen rapidly in rank from orderly to lieutenant colonel. His responsibility was that of chief quartermaster. At the annual review of troops he took pleasure in appearing in full uniform, with cocked hat, epaulets, and sword. In later years he recollected when he had "played soldier, after a fashion."[6] His commission in the militia was signed by New York Governor William H. Seward, later secretary of state under President Lincoln.

George had also made the acquaintance of Miss Sarah Catherine Wright, daughter of Judge Benjamin Wright of Adams, Massachusetts. The couple had met while decorating the Episcopal church in Watertown for Christmas worship services. Fairbanks was twenty years old at the time, she some eighteen months older and a student at a select girls' school in Adams. During the winter and spring months of 1841 George went often to Adams to visit with Sarah, and by summertime they were engaged.

The occasion of the marriage was provided by the arrival in Watertown during the summer of 1842 of Isaac H. Bronson, his wife, and two daughters. A member for some years of the Watertown law firm of Bronson and Sterling, Bronson had served in Congress during the Martin Van Buren administration, but had not been reelected. Ill health compelled him to accept appointment as judge of the United States Superior Court of East Florida, and he and his family made their home in the more congenial climate afforded by St. Augustine. In 1842 they were on a visit to Watertown, and Mrs. Bronson took a fancy to George's fiancée, Sarah Wright. By another coincidence, in September of the same year, Fairbanks' future father-in-law, Major John Beard, who had been clerk of the Superior Court at St. Augustine, was appointed United States Marshal. The clerkship fell vacant at St. Augustine, and Judge Bronson, probably at the urging of his wife, offered Fairbanks the position. The offer was gladly accepted, but George was unwilling to leave for so distant a home without completing his plans for marriage with Sarah. He therefore made arrangements for the wedding to take place before his departure, and her parents consented to the plan with the understanding that she could remain at home in Adams until the following summer, when Fairbanks would return for her. The couple were married on Saturday afternoon, October 8, 1842 in the Zion Church, Pierrepont Manor, about five miles outside Adams.[7]

A week later Fairbanks joined Judge and Mrs. Bronson, their two daughters, Gertrude and

Emma, and a party of military and civil officials in New York for a journey by ship to Savannah. One of the military officers aboard was Captain John T. Sprague, of the United States Army, who had fought in the Second Seminole War. In 1848 Sprague would publish *The Origin, Progress, and Conclusion of the Florida War*, for many years the only booklength account of that conflict.[8]

Fairbanks and his companions had a pleasant voyage down the coast, lasting, he remembered, some five or six days. After a brief stopover at the Pulaski House in Savannah, the party boarded the *Cincinnati*, a government-chartered steamboat, for the passage through the Georgia coastal islands and down the St. Johns River to the military post and landing station at Picolata, eighteen miles west of St. Augustine. It was a rough passage. A heavy gale came up en route, and the *Cincinnati* was forced to seek shelter in the St. Marys River. The captain and crew took the vessel fifteen miles up the river, searching for wood, and had to anchor overnight for fear the gale would cause the ship to be thrown up on shore. When the weather subsided somewhat, the *Cincinnati* was able to move past Jacksonville and down the St. Johns to Picolata. There the party spent the night at the home of John Lee Williams, Florida history buff and one of the two commissioners who in 1824 had recommended a site in West Florida for the seat of government for the Territory of Florida. At the recommended site the town of Tallahassee had been founded.

From Picolata, Fairbanks and his friends traveled in "hacks—a sort of ambulance conveyance" to St. Augustine, which he described shortly afterwards in a letter to his brother, Samuel, as "the oddest looking little old place you can imagine— there is not a thing in it scarcely that looks less than a hundred years old."[9] With a population of some 1,800 to 2,000 people and compactly built in the European manner, St. Augustine resembled Montreal more than any other place Fairbanks had seen. He took quarters at the Florida House on Treasury Lane, then the principal hotel, and during the four or five days he waited until the Bronsons were ready to receive him into their own pleasant home fronting the entrance to the harbor on the seawall, Fairbanks explored the town.

The larger portion of the white population, Fairbanks discovered, were Minorcans (a group name that included some of Greek, Italian, and Turkish, as well as of Minorcan, origin), descendants of the colony brought to Florida by Dr. Andrew Turnbull in 1768, five years after the cession of Florida by Spain to England. In later years, Fairbanks remembered, "The northern portion of the city was almost entirely occupied by them [Minorcans]. Some few English families from the

West Indies, the Andersons, Dummetts, etc., had
left plantations on the coast south of St. Augustine at the commencement of the Indian war and
settled in St. Augustine. Some Americans, but not
many, were living there as merchants or holding
public office. There was hardly a private carriage
in the place—the streets were narrow without
sidewalks, balconies projected from the upper
story of the two-story houses, some of the oldest
of which were built of concrete with a roof nearly
flat of concrete like the houses of Havana. The
entrance to these old houses was generally in the
yard and the living room upstairs, with no open-
ings to the north, and some without chimneys,
being heated with brasiers. In the better class [one
found] silver candlesticks with wax candles and a
glass cylinder, plain or ornamental, about two feet
in height and 8 or 10 inches [in] diameter, which
was placed over the candlestick and candle to protect it from the wind."[10]

Fairbanks discovered "a kind of aristocracy"
among the Minorcans and Spanish-speaking residents of St. Augustine: "One Pedro Benet was a
leading citizen of this class. He was a shopkeeper
and had a very good residence, on Charlotte St.
about a block or two South of the City Gates. He
was often spoken of as the Minorcan King and
was understood to very largely control his com-
patriots socially and politically."[11] The Minor-

cans and Spanish-speaking people had frequent entertainments and social functions, but there was very little mingling, Fairbanks discovered, between that group and the American population of the city.

Among the latter there were also frequent social gatherings, and wine and cakes were served. These were weekly activities, and visitors to St. Augustine for their health or for recreation were generally invited. Officers from the two companies of the Third United States Artillery stationed at Saint Francis Barracks in the south section of the city also attended. Occasionally the officers themselves hosted dances at the barracks, where music was furnished by a trio led by Marcellini, a black musician who specialized in dance music. Oyster roasts would sometimes be held by the American residents on Anastasia Island opposite the city.

Fairbanks was much struck by the variety of life in St. Augustine. Nearly all nationalities were represented in the city, which was, he averred, "in all respects unlike any American town. . . . Its varieties of inhabitants and mixture of languages gave it a peculiarly interesting character."[12] Fairbanks was particularly struck by two unique characters. The first, a Mr. Fencher, was a native of Rhode Island who had engaged in business with various concerns in Mexico and at the time of Fairbanks' arrival owned a residence and plantation on North River above St. Augustine. Fairbanks was impressed by Mr. Fencher's size, which he estimated at being over six hundred pounds in weight. As a contrast he cited Mr. Jarried Barker, who lived not far from Mr. Fencher; Mr. Barker had a fully developed body, but his legs were only a few inches in length. Barker's wife was rather tall, and Fairbanks was amused to learn that when Barker displeased her, she placed him on the mantelpiece.

As clerk of the Superior Court, Fairbanks had an office in Government House, which fronted the public square. On one side were the offices of Judge Bronson and the district attorney; on the other side that of the United States marshal. The bar at that time consisted of the Honorable Joseph L. Smith, judge (and father of the famed Confederate General Edmund Kirby-Smith), Major B. A. Putnam, John Drysdale, and O. M. Dorman, all attorneys. In a letter to his brother, Samuel, written early in November 1842, shortly after George's arrival in Florida, Fairbanks said, "I am sitting with doors open and as comfortable as in our summer months."[13]

In the summer of 1843 Fairbanks journeyed to Watertown and returned to St. Augustine that fall with his wife, Sarah. They boarded for a while with Mrs. Martha M. Reid, "a very intelligent lady," the widow of Robert Raymond Reid who had been a governor of the Territory of Florida. In June 1844 Fairbanks purchased for $300 property containing 106 acres and known as the Robinson place, one and a half miles north of the city gate, on the San Sebastian River. There was a small house on the property, "in front of which grew an ever-blooming rose which I think attracted me to the place."[14] The south boundary was popularly called "The Stockade," since it had marked the outer north line of fortifications in Spanish times and ran from the San Sebastian to the North River. That same year the Fairbanks built a cottage, "Vado Real," and it remained the family home until 1859, when Fairbanks, then a widower, left St. Augustine. During the Civil War the cottage and real property were cared for by a female slave, Venus Adams, whom Fairbanks had purchased April 1, 1846. She was then thirty years old. Vado Real was burned during the war, as Fairbanks, who was on service with the Confederate Army in Georgia, learned from a captured Union officer at Andersonville.[15]

On this same property—more precisely on a southwestern triangular portion thereof—Fairbanks would bury his wife and third child, both of whom died before his departure from St. Augustine. He explained that he did not wish to bury his family in the Roman Catholic cemetery, since it "was probably consecrated to the use of members of that church." Neither did he wish to bury them in the Protestant cemetery immediately north of the city gate (popularly called the Huguenot Cemetery) because "it had no consecration except by its use."[16] Sometime after Fairbanks left St. Augustine, he conveyed the triangular piece of property to the wardens and vestry of Trinity Parish, the Protestant Episcopal Church in the city, for use as a private burial ground.

Fairbanks interested himself in the civil and military affairs of Florida.[17] One of the residents of St. Augustine, well advanced in years, whom Fairbanks met in the course of his early career as clerk of the court, was Moses Elias Levy. Involved at the time in litigation over title to lands that he had purchased from the Arredondo estate, Levy frequently came to Fairbanks' office to examine papers and take notes. The two became friends, "as much so as an old man and young man can be," Fairbanks would relate.[18] After a brief acquaintance, Levy proposed that Fairbanks take charge of his lawsuits and land matters. The young attorney agreed and served Levy ten years as confidential advisor and agent. When the relationship ended, Levy was free of all litigation, and he had several large parcels of land, mostly in the Alachua area, and money enough to make him comfortable the balance of his life.

Moses Levy had lived a colorful life. "He occasionally talked with me concerning his previous life, and said his Father was the Grand Vizier of the Emperor of Morocco, and discovered a conspiracy on the part of the heir apparent to dethrone his father. He caused the imprisonment of the young prince and of course earned his bitter hatred. The Emperor died and the son came to the throne. The Grand Vizier placed his family in safety at Gibraltar, and fled himself to Egypt, where, I understand from Mr. Levy, his Father died."[19] Levy's family had been Portuguese Jewish refugees in Morocco, and bore the honorary Moorish title name of Yulee. Levy spent his youth in Gibraltar, and sailed as a young man to St. Thomas Island, West Indies, where he accumulated a large fortune from the lumber business. It was in St. Thomas that, finding his name too long and cumbersome for business purposes, he dropped the final cognomen of Yulee. His usual signature was simply M. E. Levy. Fairbanks obviously held him in high esteem. Writing in later life from Sewanee, Tennessee, in 1901, he remembered: "Mr. Moses E. Levy was a man universally respected in Saint Augustine. His probity, large intelligence and benevolence were by all recognized. I held him in the highest regard and veneration. He was very fond of children, who were attracted to him. He was just and generous in his business transactions. I understood, but I do not know that I ever heard him speak of it, that his purpose in buying these large bodies of lands [in Alachua] was to establish a colony of Jewish people as a refuge and religious community."[20]

Levy had two sons, Elias and David, who also distinguished themselves.[21] After education in Virginia, David returned to St. Augustine and was elected territorial delegate to Congress in 1841. The elder Levy was opposed to David's entering politics, and his opposition was taken advantage of by certain "unscrupulous politicians," in Fairbanks' terms, who sowed dissension between the son and father for political purposes. For some years there was no contact between father and son. "I was a close friend of the son," Fairbanks wrote, "and on one occasion told him the family history as had been told me by his father. He applied to the legislature [in 1846] and by an Act of Legislature took the name of David Levy Yulee—his brother Elias also changed to Yulee."[22] Soon afterwards, following David's marriage and birth of a child, Fairbanks was instrumental in effecting a reconciliation between the father and his son. In 1845, when Florida was received into the Union, David was elected by the Florida General Assembly as United States senator, the first Jew in the country's history to hold that office. The family's name is perpetuated in Florida in Levy County and in the town of Yulee.[23]

Fairbanks himself entered political life in 1846. A Jeffersonian Democrat, with important political friends, among them former Territorial Governor William P. DuVal,[24] Fairbanks ran successfully for state senator. He moved to Tallahassee for the period of his two-year term, 1846–47, and showed considerable skill as one of the fledgling state's young legislators. Only twenty-six years of age at the time, he was put in nomination for presidency of the senate and tied in the voting with the senator from Pensacola. A compromise candidate eventually won the office. In the legislature Fairbanks engaged actively in the affairs of the judiciary committee and introduced a comprehensive revenue bill. An insight into Fairbanks' mind at this period is afforded by an exchange of letters with fellow senator Samuel L. Burritt, in December 1847. The two men had disagreed on the propriety of a floor vote, and Fairbanks thought that Burritt had imputed unworthy motives to him. Writing to the latter on Christmas day, Fairbanks said: "It is a matter of pride with me that I have lived thus far with scarcely a personal disagreement and that I am unconscious at the present time of having a personal enemy in the world, but from what has passed it's necessary that there should be some better understanding between us before the intercourse which has been interrupted can be resumed with pleasure to either party. Politically we may, and probably shall, differ, but I see no necessity of carrying such differences of opinion into the relations of private life."[25] Burritt replied gracefully the next morning and apologized for the apparent imputation. "The conclusion which I drew from your proposition . . . was a hasty one," he wrote. "You disavow the intention I imputed to you. I am sorry I did impute it and I shall be happy if this mutual explanation shall have the effect to restore our former amicable relations."[26]

Following his brief term of office as senator, Fairbanks returned to St. Augustine and to the practice of law. He would not present himself as a candidate for public office again until 1853, when, with the resignation of Benjamin Putnam, the office of surveyor general of Florida fell vacant. Former Senator James D. Westcott, Jr., attempted to secure that office for his brother John, but he was vigorously opposed by David Yulee, an anti-Westcott partisan, who considered the post of surveyor general the most influential federal position in Florida. Initially, Yulee wished to see the post go to John Beard, a close friend of Fairbanks' and later the latter's father-in-law.[27] Beard would not accept the office, however, and Yulee turned to his friend Fairbanks, who agreed to run. The anti-Westcott forces gave lively support to Fairbanks and interceded on his behalf with Florida's Democratic congressional delegation, with Secretary of the Interior Robert McClelland, and with President Franklin Pierce. Senator Yulee, as might be expected, armed Fairbanks with numerous written recommendations from highly placed Florida citizens.[28] In the end, however, the efforts of Fairbanks and the anti-Westcott forces were blunted by a third candidate, Colonel Gad Humphreys, an Indian agent for Florida, who was active in Democratic politics. Humphreys and Yulee had had a falling out at the National Democratic Convention in 1852, where Humphreys broke the unanimity of a Florida delegation favorable to Stephen Douglas, apparently at the urging of John Westcott. Unaware of Humphreys' strength, Fairbanks traveled to Washington armed with his letters of introduction and talked with August Maxwell, a moderate Democrat, from whom he learned that Yulee's successor in the United States Senate, Stephen R. Mallory, was throwing his weight behind Humphreys. Fairbanks was greatly disappointed to learn this, but preferred Humphreys to Westcott and so advised Humphreys' son: "All my wishes & feelings as between Dr. Westcott and your Father are in your Father's favor and . . . I hope if there is a question as to whether your Father or Dr. Westcott shall be appointed, that it will be given to your Father."[29]

Fairbanks' next and final candidacy for office in Florida was more successful. In 1857 he was elected

mayor of St. Augustine. His inaugural speech to
city officials pointed up certain unstable features
of the community's life at that time, as well as
Fairbanks' own pro-slavery proclivities. As owner
of several slaves himself, Fairbanks cautioned his
hearers about the unruly behavior of the slave
population in the city: "They are allowed greater
liberties than they should be, and it is very evidently injurious to them. We have a great many
idle negroes, we have a great many drunken negroes, we have a great many very dishonest negroes."[30] Many blacks, Fairbanks observed, were
daily drunk in the streets and their masters had
no information as to where they obtained their al-
cohol. He also objected to the fact that blacks
were allowed by their masters to have independent
homes and a style of living that "begets a desire
for something better than rations & makes them
get up meetings at each other's houses with corresponding entertainments which somebody has to
pay for." That independent lifestyle of the blacks
in the city had, so Fairbanks complained, a bad
effect in "lessening that wholesome relation of de-
pendence of master and slave which is better for
the servant & requisite to the master's proper control."

Fairbanks also expressed his concern about the
amount of malicious mischief that had been occurring in the city, some of which he attributed to

practical joking that caused injury instead of amusement. He promised to devote his administration to the resolution of that problem and also to the more important problem occasioned by the mounting number of thefts of hen roosts, garden produce, and fruit trees. "It is a very galling thing when one has fattened his poultry and awaiting the use of it, to find it stolen without excuse and without any greater amount of cunning than possessed by very inferior instincts. So with gardens and fruit. . . . To find our property thus wantonly assailed and carried off creates a bitterness of feeling which reacts upon society at large and has & will drive many a family from making their home here so long as it exists—and it most frequently happens that these depredations are made upon defenseless women and old people not capable of protecting themselves. It is shameful that so much of this kind of thing is going on and I hope we may do something toward stopping it. It is not to be expected that people will surround their dwellings with fierce dogs or stand armed all night to keep off thieves from their hen roosts or fruit gardens."[31]

In that same year, Fairbanks and other civic leaders had to concern themselves with a growing number of Seminole Indian attacks on American settlements and travelers. He was one of a committee appointed at a meeting of citizens of St.

Augustine to secure protection.[32] Although the
Second Seminole War officially was over, there still
were small bands of Indians that attacked out-
lying settlements. The St. Augustine committee
took cognizance of one recent "massacre" of an
entire family at New Smyrna and to the "heap of
ashes and the mutilated corpses left behind." The
members drew attention to "the practice of the
wily Indian foe whenever hard pressed to scatter
through the country under cover of the swamps &
familiar passes and suddenly commit attacks."[33]
They urged Brigadier General William S. Harney,
commanding the United States forces in Florida,
to raise a mounted company of soldiers to scout
the country between St. Augustine and the St.
Johns River and to assure the safety of the stage
and public mail route between St. Augustine and
Picolata.[34]

It was in the 1850s, apparently, that Fairbanks
first developed his interest in history, particularly
that of Florida. The first indication of that interest
is found in a letter to Fairbanks from Professor
Theodore Irving of Free Academy in New York.
Irving, then revising his *The Conquest of Florida
by Hernando de Soto*,[35] wrote asking for any information that Fairbanks might have on the early
Spanish explorations in Florida, and he expressed
the hope that, "thorough search might bring to light
something which might remove a great deal of the

mist that obscures the early history of your state. . . ."[36] One supposes, on the basis of this communication, that Fairbanks' name had been given to Irving as one who was interested in the Spanish period of Florida history.

Perhaps the general quietude into which St. Augustine was settling in the 1850s also contributed to Fairbanks' interest in the past. The long Second Seminole War had ended and with it St. Augustine's bustling activity as a military post. Once the leading city in Florida, by 1855 it had fallen to fifth place in population. An English traveler, Lady Amelia Murray, described the city as "in general appearance . . . bare and dilapidated."[37] Writing to his children, John Beard complained about the bleakness surrounding St. Augustine in the 1850s, saying: "This poor old place is so much depressed that it is impossible to describe the change from what it was when we first knew it. You can perceive everywhere, and in everything, both animate and inanimate, the melancholy vestiges of adversity. But amid all this ruin I find still much cheerfulness, and among our old friends undiminished cordiality."[38]

Fairbanks' own description of the community during the same period can be found by the reader in this present volume, pages 9-10: "And yet about the old city there clings a host of historic associations, which throw around it a charm which few can fail to feel." It was these things which interested Fairbanks during the 1850s. He mastered the Spanish language, according to his son-in-law, so that he could read the history of the early Florida explorations and settlements in the language of the original adventurers.[39]

In 1855 Fairbanks and a group of like-minded men gathered in the upstairs hall of George Burt's St. Augustine store, a place often used for public gatherings, and discussed the organization of a society that would promote historical studies, not only of St. Augustine, but of the entire state. Early in 1856 the planners, together with a number of other leading Florida citizens, met again and formally organized "The Historical Society of Florida." A constitution and bylaws were adopted and officers were elected. Major Benjamin A. Putnam was elected president; Fairbanks, McQueen McIntosh, David Levy Yulee, William A. Forward, and the Reverend J. H. Myers, were named vice-presidents; George Burt became corresponding secretary and treasurer; K. B. Gibbs, recording secretary and librarian; and the Reverend A. A. Miller, C. M. Dorman, and Father Edmond Aubril were elected to the executive committee.[40]

By April 1857 there were 134 members in the society, including many of the outstanding men in Florida politics. At the quarterly meeting of the society held that same month in Government

House at St. Augustine, Fairbanks delivered a lecture which is the first known historical essay from his hand. Entitled "The Early History of Florida," the lecture was a survey of exploration and settlement in Florida from the time of the first voyage of Ponce de León (dated erroneously in 1512 according to the common understanding of the time) up to the period of the English settlement in Georgia and Carolina in the seventeenth and eighteenth centuries.[41]

The lecture in printed form filled twenty-four pages. In it Fairbanks said that he could do no more with so short a space than to glance rapidly at the more prominent points of Florida's early history. "My aim has been rather to indicate that we have a history, replete with interest, extending back to the earliest of American discoveries."[42] Standing within the walls of what he called "The Palace of the Spanish Governors," Fairbanks said: "This most ancient city of our land, within the shadow of that gray and moss-covered castle, where everything recalls the past, whose very existence is a landmark of history [provokes] an earnest desire to look into that past, to draw out its secrets, and to bring back to our own minds and memories the scenes and actions of the olden time; and when our day shall in its turn be numbered with the past, and others shall have succeeded us, as we now fill the places of the generations who on this spot have been born and died, it may well be that a tribute of affectionate respect and reverence may be then bestowed upon us, as the founders and benefactors of this Society."[43] The society, he said, planned to explore Florida's past, to keep and preserve all that could be discovered in trust for those who would follow afterwards, to build a library which would be open for reference to scholars, teachers, and students, to collect all relevant manuscript and published works relating to Florida's history, and by means of lectures and publications to communicate that history to the general population.

The historical portion of the lecture is sketchy and uneven, with several misspellings of Spanish names. There are questionable facts and numerous omissions, e.g., the settlement of Tristán de Luna at Pensacola in 1559–62. Still, it is as good a short essay on Spanish exploration and settlement of Florida as could be found at the time, and its felicitous style makes for easy reading, as it must, in 1857, have pleased the ears and sensibilities of the society members who heard it. Indeed, it may be said that, except for chapter one of the present book to which these pages are an introduction, there is no part of *History and Antiquities* that can equal the *Introductory Lecture* for both style and historic insight. Fully eight pages out of the nineteen given to Florida's early Spanish history

Fairbanks devoted to the conflict between the Spaniards and French at Fort Caroline, St. Augustine, and Matanzas Inlet in 1565 and 1568. The latter was the year of the avenging assault on Fort Caroline (renamed San Mateo) by Dominique de Gourgues. This disproportionate rendering of the history also characterizes the *History and Antiquities*, where ninety-five of two hundred pages are devoted to the same subject. Of Fairbanks' attitude toward the Spanish-French struggle more will be said later.

The good reception of his lecture, in both its oral and published forms, caused Fairbanks to project a book on the same theme, with a concentration on St. Augustine. To that end he entered upon a correspondence with his St. Augustine friend, Thomas Buckingham Smith, who at that time was secretary of the United States legation in Madrid, Spain. There is no full-length biography of Smith, whose name, like that of Fairbanks, is closely associated with the story of St. Augustine in the nineteenth century; but the essential facts of his life, so far as they relate to the present study, may be set forth as follows.[44] Ten years older than Fairbanks, Smith had been born October 31, 1810 on Cumberland Island, Georgia, the son of Josiah Smith and Hannah Smith (cousins) of Watertown, Connecticut. The family established itself in St. Augustine some time shortly afterwards, and Smith appears to have spent most of his boyhood in the old Florida city. At the age of fourteen he visited Mexico, where his father had been appointed United States consul. The following year, 1825, his father died, and Smith became the ward of an uncle, Robert Smith, of New Bedford, Massachusetts, who sent him to Trinity College in Hartford, Connecticut, for three years. Afterwards he attended Harvard Law School, from which he graduated in 1836. After a short time working in a Portland, Maine, law office, Smith returned to St. Augustine in 1839, and began a law practice that would last eleven years. During that period, he served as secretary to Governor Reid (1839–40), as a member of the St. Augustine city council, and as a member of the territorial legislature (1841). On September 20, 1844 Smith married Julia B. Gardiner of Concord, New Hampshire.

While practicing law in St. Augustine, Smith developed an interest in historical research, particularly in the area of Spanish explorations and settlements in North America. Perhaps it was his interest that would later influence his friend Fairbanks to pursue the same studies. The earliest extant record of Smith's research in the Spanish period is found in an unpublished manuscript of twenty-four pages entitled "Annals of Florida," preserved in the Library of Congress. A notation on the manuscript, not in Smith's hand, states:

"Written about 1835-6." That date would coincide
with Smith's final year at Harvard. The "Annals"
is a highly stylized account, undocumented, of the
discovery of Florida by Ponce de León in 1512
(again the erroneous date) and continuing as far
as 1525. Appended to the "Annals" are seven manuscript pages copied from correspondence of Spanish Governor Manuel de Montiano (1737-49) from
the "Archives of Saint Augustine, Florida," copied
by Elias B. Gould of St. Augustine. The description of the letters, thirty-six in all and addressed
to the Captain-General of Cuba, is given in Smith's
own hand.[45] Fairbanks would make use of those
letters in the present work, spelling the governor's
name "Monteano" (see pp. 142-50 passim).

Smith's increasing interest in the Spanish presence in North America, particularly in Florida, led
him to seek an appointment as secretary to the
United States legation at Mexico City, which,
through the influence of Senator Jackson Morton,
he secured on September 9, 1850. His sole purpose, apparently, in obtaining this assignment was
to gain access to the Spanish archives. He spent
his time well, copying ancient manuscripts to
which Mexican authorities gave him free and full
use, and scouring the countryside for books and
papers that he might bring back to Mexico City
on muleback and send to such American historians
as Peter Force, Jared Sparks, George Bancroft,

Francis Parkman, William Prescott, and Henry R. Schoolcraft. It is not recorded that Fairbanks was favored by Smith in the same manner, and it is improbable that he would be, since Smith's tenure at Mexico City antedated Fairbanks' known interest in historical studies.

Smith returned to the United States in 1852, and for the next three years spent his time equally between St. Augustine and Washington, writing and publishing historical articles and seeking a new appointment as secretary to the legation at Madrid, where the most abundant store of Spanish Florida materials could be found. To a friend Smith wrote in 1853: "I tell you plainly I am going to Spain and at my own expense if necessary, should no pleasanter means present itself."[46] Finally on June 9, 1855 Smith received the desired appointment and departed for Europe the same year, where he researched and copied manuscripts in the archives of Madrid and in the other and more abundant collections of Seville and Simancas.[47]

This period of Smith's life and work, 1855–58, established him as the first American scholar to collect and copy documentary materials for the history of Florida from archives in Spain. The result of his efforts was a prodigious collection of documents, copied personally or through the agency of others, the greater portion of which is now in the library of the New York Historical Society, to which Smith bequeathed the collection. Altogether, the materials fill twenty-five volumes, large and small, and consist of full copies of early Spanish contracts, memorials, reports, and correspondence, tracings or copies of early Florida maps, and miscellaneous papers relating to linguistics, geography, and ethnology, all from the period 1500–1800.

While in Spain, Smith made preparations for the publication of his transcripts. However, only one volume of source materials on Florida and adjacent areas was issued, and that in 1857.[48] This would have been in time for Fairbanks to use had it reached his hands, although it is doubtful that it did so, because there is no trace of these documents in the present book. Certainly, one supposes that Fairbanks would have utilized Smith's published transcript of Philip II's grant of the title *adelantado* of Florida, to Pedro Menéndez de Avilés, as presumably he would also have used other of the documents relating to the founding years of St. Augustine and Florida, e.g., the will of Pedro Menéndez Marqués, nephew and heir to the adelantado, who governed in St. Augustine;[50] a 1758 report of the governor at St. Augustine on the poor conditions prevailing at that time in the Florida colony;[51] and, perhaps also, a report by Juan de la Vandera on the findings of the expedition of Juan Pardo into the interior of South Carolina during the year immediately following the foundation of St. Augustine.[52] In the extant letters from Smith to Fairbanks, dated 1858, there is no mention by Smith of this collection.[53] Indeed, it appears that the extent to which Smith contributed to this present volume is represented in the engravings of Fort Caroline (p. 28) and of Pedro Menéndez de Avilés (p. 109). In the publisher's advertisement for *History and Antiquities*, the Menéndez engraving is described as coming from a "newly-discovered portrait."[54] It was for this service, apparently—as well as for reasons of friendship and influence—that Fairbanks graciously dedicated the book to Smith and paid his published thanks for his "repeated favors" in the course of its preparation.[55]

This productive period of Smith's life came to an end in 1858, the year of his correspondence with Fairbanks, owing to personal conflicts with the minister of the legation, Augustus L. Dodge of Iowa.[56] Smith returned to the United States with a treasure-trove of books and transcripts of documents. He was back in St. Augustine by 1860, but after the outbreak of the Civil War he moved to New York City. Although a slaveowner, he sided with the Union during that conflict, and in May 1864 he was a delegate to the Democratic Convention in Baltimore, Maryland.

Following the war, Smith traveled again to Spain, where he continued his investigations in the archives of Seville and Simancas, and selected improved stocks for the orange groves that he maintained in St. Augustine. In 1868 he returned to Florida and was appointed tax commissioner. In 1870–71 he was again in New York City, where on January 4, 1871 he suffered a stroke near his home at 261 West 42nd Street, and collapsed on the sidewalk. Thinking that Smith was intoxicated, a policeman hauled him off to the police station and locked him in a cell overnight. In the morning he was taken to Bellevue Hospital, where he died. His remains were moved to the city morgue, and they were about to be consigned to a pauper's grave when a banker-acquaintance identified them and arranged to have them sent south to St. Augustine, where they were placed in the so-called Huguenot Cemetery.

Smith's will was later discovered in the safe of a St. Augustine merchant. Dated July 15, 1869, it bequeathed all his historical manuscripts to the New York Historical Society, "with this reservation, that during the lifetime of John Gilmary Shea they be for his consultation & none other & for such use may be withdrawn from the custody of the society any of them."[57] Shea, noted historian of the Catholic Church in the United States, composed a memoir of Smith which included a bibliography of his published works, both of which appeared as an introduction to Smith's translation of Alvar Nuñez Cabeça de Vaca, published in 1871.[58]

Most of his personal wealth Smith left "for the use of the black people of St. Augustine and their successors in all time to come . . . providing first for the aged and invalid of those blacks which have been mine."[59] As a sign of his concern for his former servants, Smith left his orange grove and residence on the banks of Maria Sanchez Creek to "the negro Jack—once my slave."[60] In consequence of these bequests, the Buckingham Smith Benevolent Association was founded in 1873 and perdures to this date as an agency of assistance to the black people of St. Augustine.

Fairbanks described this present work, *History and Antiquities*, as having "grown out of a lecture delivered by the author," which would have been, of course, the *Introductory Lecture* to the Historical Society of Florida. In point of fact, however, there is nothing in the present volume of the original lecture, save names, facts, and dates, and all these are rendered in entirely different language. It may be asked, what were Fairbanks' sources? We have seen above that he did not use Buckingham Smith's transcripts. A close reading of the text reveals that the bulk of the work (123 pages out of the total of 200) is a condensed translation of the *Ensayo Cronológico para la Historia Ge-*

neral de la Florida, written in the eighteenth century by Andrés González de Barcia Carballido y Zúñiga (under the anagram Don Gabriel de Cardenas z Cano).[61] Much of the narrative Fairbanks quotes from Barcia *in extenso*, it being his aim, he states in the preface (p. 5), to preserve the style and quaintness of the writers from whom he drew his information. Barcia was little known in St. Augustine and Florida at that time, and Fairbanks no doubt performed a valuable scholarly service in translating much of its pertinent East Florida material.

His account of the foundation of St. Augustine and of the contest between the Spaniards and the French is drawn in the main from two sources: the "Memorial" of Gonzalo Solís de Merás, brother-in-law of Menéndez and chronicler of the 1565 expedition, as found in Barcia;[62] and the "Memorial" of Menéndez' fleet chaplain, Francisco López de Mendoza Grajales,[63] which Fairbanks had in a published French translation by Henri Ternaux-Compans.[64] He also utilized the correspondence of Governor Manuel de Montiano with the Captain-General of Cuba (1737–41). The same correspondence had been used by Buckingham Smith in his short essay, "Annals of Florida," but there is no indication that Fairbanks depended upon Smith for these documents, which were readily available to him in the East Florida archives preserved in the governor's house at St. Augustine.[65]

Fairbanks' other sources for this history, together with the page numbers of the present volume where each can be found either used or referred to, may be listed as follows: Nicolas le Challeux,[66] 36–50; Jacques le Moyne de Morgues,[67] 50, 54; René Goulaine de Laudonnière,[68] 52–54; Dominique de Gourgues,[69] 102–7; Bartholomew Rivers Carroll,[70] 127 ff.; William James Rivers,[71] 127 ff.; William Gilmore Simms,[72] 51–52; William Roberts,[73] 159; William Bartram,[74] 159; William Stork,[75] 159; Bernard Romans,[76] 159; William Gerard De Brahm,[77] 164–68; John Lee Williams,[78] 168, 186; the anonymous author of *Narrative of a Voyage to the Spanish Main*,[79] 176–82; and William Cullen Bryant,[80] 191–200. Some of these source books may have been sent to Fairbanks by Buckingham Smith, since one does not suppose at this time the existence of an extensive Floridiana library at St. Augustine, but there is no evidence that he sent them. In any event, Fairbanks can be credited with being the first American historian of Florida to make major use of the Spanish records, particularly of the then little known Barcia history; and his synthesis within a single compact volume of most of the known published works on Florida of Spanish, French, English, and American origin also had a particular value for the time. Although his sometimes overly long extracts from the writers impeded the smoothness of the narrative, no doubt many readers were more pleased to have original texts in the English language than they would have been to have the writer's narrative alone. Despite its sketchy and uneven character, this history of St. Augustine was without question the best summary of its kind written to that date.[81]

As noted earlier, ninety-five of Fairbanks' two hundred pages (pp. 15–110) are devoted to the conflict between the Spaniards and the French in their endeavors to secure hegemony over Florida during the years 1564–68. The unusual emphasis on the events of four years out of the nearly three hundred surveyed in this volume reveals Fairbanks' fascination with the bloody duel of Pedro Menéndez de Avilés, that "brave, bigoted, and remorseless soldier," as Fairbanks calls him (p. 17), with the adelantado's French counterparts, Jean Ribault, René de Laudonnière, and Dominique de Gourgues. Fairbanks' exaggerated treatment of those events may be said, furthermore, to have contributed one reason why readers of American history have tended to associate Menéndez' name with the *leyenda negra*—the "black legend" image of Spaniards as cruel, deceitful, bigoted, and greedy. In particular, Fairbanks was concerned to

show that Menéndez acted with inexcusable barbarity and, what was worse, dishonorable deception in his massacre of Ribault's Frenchmen at
Matanzas Inlet (pp. 65–90). Three years after that
"monstrous atrocity" (p. 90), the punitive expedi-
tionary force of French Captain de Gourgues fell
upon the Spanish occupiers of Fort Caroline and
put them to the sword with the same *sang-froid*
exhibited by Menéndez. Fairbanks' comparison
of the two massacres leaves the reader no doubt
that he regarded the Spaniard as villain of the
piece, and his faint censure of Gourgues' "violation of the pure spirit of . . . Christianity" (p. 107)
is plainly outweighed by his sympathetic recital
of the Frenchman's understandable, if not, indeed,
virtuous motivation. Interestingly, Fairbanks re-
sponded to Gourgues' actions with far less forbear-
ance in the *Introductory Lecture* of 1857, where
he said: "I know nothing in history more peculiar,
more tragic, than this scheme of vengeance for a
national wrong, conceived, planned, and carried
into effect by Gourgues. Laying aside the ordinary
motives which prompt mankind to action, sternly
bending his whole life, energy, and being into one
sanguinary work, from which he was to derive no
benefit, no reward, and perchance punishment and
disgrace, we are awed by the sternness of such a
character."[82]

No doubt the one isolated and terrible incident

at Matanzas will forever stain the otherwise admirable breastplate of Menéndez. Indeed, there were already some at St. Augustine in 1565, Solís de Merás tells us, who "considered him cruel," while others determined that "he had acted as a very good captain should."[83] Most of the serious historical literature on the subject since the time of Fairbanks' book has tended to mix the two judgments reported by Merás, and to find justification, in one measure or another, for the severity of Menéndez' tactics. One should not wish to overdraw the revisionism that has taken place on this point, but it is worth observing that the two most recently published accounts of the Matanzas affair are markedly understanding of Menéndez and of the position in which he found himself vis-à-vis the French forces. Whether this shift in view bespeaks a transition from nineteenth-century historiographical idealism to a more pragmatic and situation-ethical approach to human events is problematical, but a sampling of the most respected twentieth-century interpreters, presented here in a note, may assist the reader to come to his own balanced judgment of the rightness or wrongness of Menéndez' actions.[84] Fairbanks himself says in his preface to the present work that, in the main, he has deliberately followed the Spanish rather than the French accounts of the Matanzas episode, "desiring," he says, "to divest the narra-

tive of all suspicion of prejudice or unfairness"
(p. 6); but the reader may find, after examination
of other opinions, that the divestiture does not
succeed quite as well as Fairbanks intended.

The only other section of this narrative in which
Fairbanks took a special and personal interest was
the exact geographical location of Fort Caroline,
which he placed at St. Johns Bluff (p. 57) and designated on a map, "Entrance of Saint Johns River"
(p. 51). His judgment on the point has since been
validated by other historians and by the National
Park Service, United States Department of the
Interior, which in 1952–53 conducted extensive
archeological investigations at that site.[85] In the
second edition of *History and Antiquities*, published in 1868 (see below), Fairbanks included a
letter from Buckingham Smith in Madrid to
printer Columbus Drew in Jacksonville, under
the date August 15, 1866, in which Smith spoke
of three copper coins he discovered near the old
site of Fort Caroline and of his difficulty in obtaining their identification in London, Paris, and Spain.
He wrote: "I have visited the town of Avilés, a
league from the Bay of Biscay, whence Pedro Menéndez came, and brought his fleet to Florida
three centuries ago. I saw his tomb, and not far
off the chapel of the family of one of his companions. There is no stranger anywhere to be heard
of in all that country; everything is intensely old

Spanish in every respect. Going home late one evening, I was accosted by a native in good English. He said the town was rarely visited—three or four Englishmen within his memory had passed through, and he supposed me to be the first person from the United States who had ever been there. I told him I came from Florida, and, though rather late, was returning the visit of Menéndez to Saint Augustine." Smith went on to describe how, through the courtesy of a lineal descendant of Menéndez, the Count of Revilla Gigedo, he was permitted to read and to make copies of original Menéndez papers in the Count's possession.

The 1858 edition of *History and Antiquities* was published in New York City by Charles B. Norton, "Agent for Libraries." The actual printing was done by Baker and Godwin, Dr., Steam Printing Establishment, in the same city, at a cost of $615.55 for 750 copies, including six gift copies bound in antique library style and one copy bound in full calf leather.[86] The engraving entitled "Public Square, St. Augustine" (frontispiece), which shows the Roman Catholic Church (now Cathedral) of St. Augustine, and on the right, Trinity Episcopal Church, was done from a painting by George Harvey of Westchester County, New York, in 1854. The engraving entitled "City Gates, St. Augustine" (p. 190) came from the same hand. All the lithographic stones used for printing the illustrations in the 1858 edition were destroyed by fire in New York City some time before 1860.[87]

The original printing sold out before the onset of the Civil War and, following that conflagration, Fairbanks in 1868 brought out a second edition under the title *The Spaniards in Florida: Comprising the Notable Settlement of the Huguenots in 1864 and the History and Antiquities of St. Augustine, Founded A.D. 1565.*[88] The new edition differed little from the original, except that it was more appropriately titled, since the events recounted in the volume concerned more of East Florida than St. Augustine alone. The author was described on the title page as "Honorary Member of the New York Historical Society" and "Lecturer on American History in the University of the South." The latter institution, at Sewanee, Tennessee, had opened to students that same year, largely through the vision and energy of Fairbanks himself, as noted below. The second edition carried a new chapter 19 entitled "St. Augustine in Its Old Age, 1565–1868," in which Fairbanks surveyed the general story that he had told in the prior chapters and devoted six short paragraphs to a lamentation over the physical destruction and demoralized citizenry left at St. Augustine in the wake of the recently concluded Civil War. Among the destruction Fairbanks counted Vado Real: "A once pleasant cottage home, near the stockades, dear to the writer, cared for and embellished with many things pleasant to the eye, fragrant with the ever-blooming roses and honeysuckles, has, under the rude hand of war, been utterly destroyed, with its library, its furniture, and all its pleasant surroundings." As though handing St. Augustine to the ages, Fairbanks concluded his chapter with the sentiment: "I am sure that no one will feel otherwise than that its old age shall be tranquil and serene, and that its name may ever be associated with pleasant memories."[89]

A third and last edition, in 1881, appeared at a time when the city was gaining great favor as a tourist attraction and health resort. The title was again slightly altered, this time to read: *History and Antiquities of St. Augustine, Florida, Founded September 8, 1565.*[90] The third edition contained no new material.

The work's ranking as serious historical literature is attested to by the use made of it in later years in larger and more substantial histories, such as those written by William Whitwell Dewhurst and Charles Bingham Reynolds.[91] Fairbanks himself made extensive use of his book's material in a more comprehensive study published in 1871 under the title *History of Florida from Its Discovery by Ponce de León in 1512 to the Close of the Florida War in 1842.*[92] This work, which Fairbanks projected as the first "connected history" of the state, was primarily a factual and descriptive history almost exclusively concerned with military and political events. It was ill balanced chronologically, with marked overemphasis on three episodes: the expedition of Hernando de Soto (1539–43); the Spanish-French struggle (1564–68), which he described less passionately than he did in his earlier work; and the Second Seminole War (1835–42). Still, it was the first satisfactory history of Florida; and, just as *History and Antiquities* had introduced him as the premier historian of St. Augustine, so *History of Florida* established him as the acknowledged authority on Florida history in general. The *History of Florida* went through two further editions, in 1898 and 1904, the latter of which was issued as a textbook "with questions in appendix" for use in the Florida school system. Fairbanks was eighty-four years old at the time of the last printing.[93]

This is not the place to introduce or to analyze Fairbanks' general history, which may itself be printed in facsimile at some future date. Nor is it now possible to describe in any detail his life and activities during the Civil War or his years as cofounder, lecturer, and administrator at the University of the South. These events, which came after the original publication date of the volume before us, await the treatment of a full-length biography.[94] A brief overview of those events would show that, upon Florida's secession from the Union in 1861, Fairbanks threw in his lot with the Confederacy, and from 1862 until the end of the war he served in the commissary department of the Army of Tennessee with headquarters at Marietta, Atlanta, and Macon, Georgia. He held the rank of major throughout that period, and employed the title afterwards in private life, according to a custom popular in the South. All through his adult life he was an ardent and participating member of the Protestant Episcopal Church and attended continuously from 1853 the general conventions of that body, save during the war years when he was a delegate to the Confederate Church Council. At the convention of 1904, in Boston, he was singled out as the oldest representative at that meeting, never having once failed in attendance during a long, devoted life.

It was in connection with his Episcopal Church interests that, on July 4, 1857, Fairbanks gathered with other church leaders, clerical and lay, at Lookout Mountain, Tennessee, to organize the beginnings of the University of the South at Sewanee, projected as a regional institution of higher learning, under Episcopal auspices, for students from ten southern states. He left St. Augustine in 1859 and built a cottage, called "Rainsford Place," at Sewanee in 1860. The opening of the university was delayed by the war, and Fairbanks' cottage was burned by Federal troops in 1863. He returned to Sewanee in 1866, and he and Charles Todd Quintard, bishop of Tennessee, built log houses side by side as a sign of their determination to give the university a new birth. Both men were of northern birth and education—Quintard from Connecticut, Fairbanks from New York. Yet Fairbanks named his new home "Rebel's Rest," and it stands to this day. From 1867 until 1880, when the first two stone structures were erected, Fairbanks was University Commissioner of Land and Buildings. In the latter year he returned to Florida, taking up residence at Fernandina, where he built a handsome house, though he remained on the university's Board of Trustees. For a time, at David Levy Yulee's persuasion, he edited a weekly newspaper, *The Florida Mirror*. From Fernandina he also oversaw his extensive properties in Alachua County and helped organize the state's citrus growers. In 1903 he was elected president of the revived Florida Historical Society.

His long and distinguished scholarly career was again recognized when the University of Alabama, in June 1906, awarded him the honorary degree, Doctor of Laws. It was two months afterwards, at Sewanee, in the eighty-seventh year of his life, and shortly after exercising his position as counselor and advisor to the university he loved, that Fairbanks went to bed for the last time in his mountain home, the log house hewn out so many years before from the surrounding forest. The day of his death was August 3, 1906. Of him a colleague wrote shortly afterwards: "He was not always agreed to or listened to; he was not always understood or appreciated; it goes without saying that he was not always right in his opinions or positions"; but he was, withal, his eulogist said, "the patriarch of Sewanee, the conserver of its traditions, the exemplar of its undying faith. . . . He was the builder of it and the author of every change that it has undergone in its eventful history. . . . There is nothing here that does not and will not feel and mourn his loss."[95]

A later generation in Florida will remember him principally as Florida's first serious historian in the English language, without rival in the nineteenth century, and still deserving of our respectful notice in the twentieth.

MICHAEL V. GANNON

University of Florida

NOTES.

1. There is no satisfactory published biography of George Fairbanks. Many short sketches of his life exist, as for example: John Bell Henneman and William Porcher DuBose, "George Rainsford Fairbanks," *Sewanee Review* (October 1906), pp. 493–503; Andrew Van Vranken Raymond, *Union University* (New York: Lewis Publishing Co., 1907), vol. 3, pp. 202–4; and Francis P. Fleming, "Major George Rainsford Fairbanks," *Florida Historical Quarterly* (April 1908), pp. 5–7. They are all short in length, many of them obituary in character, and make little or no use of Fairbanks' personal papers. Those papers, now in the possession of his granddaughter, Mrs. Thomas E. Dudney (Rainsford Fairbanks Glass Dudney) of Sewanee, Tennessee, have been photocopied and the copies placed in the Special Collections Division of the Robert Strozier Library, Florida State University, Tallahassee. The present writer wishes to express his deep appreciation to Mrs. Dudney, who provided him valuable information about Fairbanks' family, as well as other life facts not available in the seventy-three folios of papers, and to the Special Collections librarians at Florida State University, who accorded him every courtesy and assistance during his research at that institution in August and September 1973. Special thanks are also due Mrs. Ann Carlin, who typed the manuscript, and Miss Nancy Mitchell, who assisted with the index.

2. His three brothers were Samuel (1818–81), Andrew Jackson (1826–98?), and Jason Massey (1828–94).

3. "Autobiographical Sketch," an 11-pp. typescript, n.d., covering events in Fairbanks' life from birth until 1846, where it ends abruptly; Fairbanks Papers (hereafter cited as F.P.), folio 1.

4. Ibid.

5. Ibid.

6. Ibid.

7. George and Sarah (February 19, 1818–March 22, 1858) would have five children: Florida (July 24, 1848–November 25, 1931); Charles Massey (April 4, 1850–February 23, 1881); George Ward (March 5, 1852–January 15, 1853); Gertrude (April 27, 1854–May 27, 1893); and Sarah Catherine (February 11, 1858–January 6, 1918).

8. John T. Sprague, *The Origin, Progress, and Conclusion of the Florida War* (New York: D. Appleton & Co., 1848); same, facsimile ed. (Gainesville: University of Florida Press, 1964). It was superseded by John K. Mahon, *History of the Second Seminole War, 1835–1842* (Gainesville: University of Florida Press, 1967).

9. F.P., folio 73, George R. Fairbanks to Samuel Fairbanks, St. Augustine, November 5, 1842.

10. F.P., folio 1, "Autobiographical Sketch."

11. Ibid.

12. Ibid.

13. F.P., folio 73, Fairbanks to Samuel Fairbanks, St. Augustine, November 5, 1842.

14. F.P., folio 1, "Autobiographical Sketch." The site is known today as the McMillan Subdivision, the southern boundary of which is 100 feet south of Harding Street.

15. F.P., folio 35, George Couper Gibbs to George Fairbanks, Andersonville, Ga., February 7, 1865.

16. F.P., folio 23, Fairbanks to Mrs. Eliza Vedder, Sewanee, Tenn., June 30, 1901. On April 26, 1860, in Chicago, Fairbanks married Susan Beard Wright (September 8, 1826–January 5, 1911), daughter of John Beard (see below, n. 27) and widow of the Reverend Benjamin Wright. Two children were born of the marriage: Susan Rainsford (July 19, 1861–October 30, 1885) and Eva Lee (March 29, 1865–September 29, 1952).

17. In the period 1844 through 1859, when he departed Florida, Fairbanks served as aide-de-camp to the governor of Florida with the rank and title of colonel. He also held the following judicial positions: master in chancery in the District of East Florida, appointed November 4, 1844; attorney, solicitor, and counselor in the several courts of the Territory of Florida, appointed March 12, 1845; master in chancery for the East Circuit of the state of Florida, appointed January 26, 1846; commissioner of common schools of the state of Florida, appointed January 7, 1847; clerk of the Court of the Northern District of Florida at the city of St. Augustine, appointed November 23, 1848; commissioner of deeds for the Court of Claims, Washington, D.C., appointed July 21, 1855; clerk of the District Court of the United States for the Northern District of Florida, appointed June 20, 1856; attorney and counselor of the Supreme Court of the United States, appointed February 3, 1857; commissioner of deeds for the state of New York in the state of Florida, appointed November 7, 1857. Fairbanks also served during this period as state senator and mayor of St. Augustine.

18. F.P., folio 51, Fairbanks to A. M. DaCosta, Sewanee, Tenn., July 1, 1901.

19. Ibid.

20. Ibid.

21. David Levy Yulee was delegate to the United States Congress from Florida (1841–45), United States senator from Florida (1845–51,

1855–61), member of the Confederate Congress (1861–65), and a pioneer railroad builder of Florida.

22. F. P., folio 51, Fairbanks to DaCosta, Sewanee, July 1, 1901.

23. Not everyone was pleased by David's change to Yulee. William P. DuVal, who had served as the first civil governor of Florida (1822–34), and was a friend and frequent correspondent of Fairbanks, complained in a letter to the latter, under the date of January 6, 1846: "The application of Mr. Levy to the Legislature to change his name to *EULIE* has given offense to many of his warmest friends—the devotion of several influential men who have hitherto maintained his pretensions and who have named there [sic] sons David Levy are seriously offended and mortified that the name is changed—I do not see any good reason why Mr. Levy should not assume his family cognomen—but trifles light as air will sometimes produce strange results"; F.P., folio 47–C, DuVal to Fairbanks, Tallahassee, January 6, 1846. David himself wrote to Fairbanks, under the same date: "By mistake my memorial to the legislature said E. instead of Y. in spelling Yulee. . . . I have a right to spell it as I please. It conforms better to my father's spelling"; F.P., folio 34, Yulee to Fairbanks, Washington, D.C., January 6, 1846. David's own account of his alienation from his father (1837) and their reconciliation (1845) is found in the David Levy Yulee Papers, P. K. Yonge Library of Florida History, University of Florida, Box 1, "Administration of M. E. Levy Estate."

24. See the correspondence between DuVal and Fairbanks, F.P., folio 60.

25. F.P., folio 60, Fairbanks to S. L. Burritt, Tallahassee, December 5, 1847.

26. F.P., folio 50, Burritt to Fairbanks, Tallahassee, December 26, 1847.

27. John Beard (1797–1876) was a North Carolinian by birth, educated at Yale, who had served as a Federalist in the North Carolina legislature before moving to St. Augustine in 1838. From that time until 1845 he held the offices of clerk of the Superior Court, in which Fairbanks replaced him in 1842, and United States marshal. On the admission of Florida to the Union in 1845, Beard was elected register of public lands and moved to Tallahassee. He ran unsuccessfully as a Democrat for Congress in 1850. He was then elected comptroller of the state, an office that he resigned in 1854 to accept the agency of the Apalachicola Land Company. He was a representative from Leon County to the secession convention of 1861, and supported the cause of the Confederacy during the course of the Civil War. At war's end he was reappointed to the office of comptroller in 1866. Three years later he was incapacitated by "vertigo" and "neuralgia," and was relatively inactive until his death in Tallahassee at eighty years of age.

Beard and Fairbanks remained close friends from the time of their first acquaintance. Not only in politics, but in the affairs of the Protestant Episcopal Church, they made common cause, often attending together various general conferences of that religious body. See Joseph D. Cushman, Jr., *A Goodly Heritage: The Episcopal Church in Florida, 1821–1892* (Gainesville: University of Florida Press, 1965), passim. After the death of his wife, Sarah, in 1858, Fairbanks in 1860 married Beard's daughter, Susan Beard Wright, widow of the Reverend Benjamin Wright.

28. An account of Fairbanks' candidacy is given in Arthur Lynch, "Patronage, Factionalism, and Sectionalism in the Florida Democratic Party, 1848–1851" (master's thesis, San Jose State College, 1969), pp. 22–24. The present writer is indebted to Mr. Lynch for this account, kindly sent him on request. See the recommendations of Fairbanks from Beard et al., in F.P., folio 60.

29. F.P., folio 60, Fairbanks to F. C. Humphreys, Washington, D.C., March 15, 1853.

30. F.P., folio 50, "Address of George R. Fairbanks to St. Augustine City Council, 1857."

31. Ibid.

32. The members of the committee, besides Fairbanks, were Colonel Gad Humphreys, F. P. Ferreira, Pedro Benet, John C. Canova, John Usina, Colonel R. F. Floyd, George Zelenbam, Bartolo Pacetty [sic], Sr. and Jr., R. D. Fontane, Luis Drysdale, William Meyes, Bartolo Pons [sic], and James Pellicer. See F.P., folio 50, "Report of Committee," December 3, 1857.

33. Ibid.

34. F.P., folio 50, "Report of Committee," with resolutions and communication to Brigadier General Harney, December 3, 1857.

35. Philadelphia: Carey, Lea & Blanchard, 1835.

36. F.P., folio 63, Theodore Irving to Fairbanks, New York, February 8, 1850.

37. Amelia M. Murray, *Letters from the United States, Cuba, and Canada* (New York: G. Putnam & Co., 1856), p. 224.

38. F.P., folio 60, John Beard to "My dear children" (Sarah and Charles), St. Augustine, July 29, 1850.

39. F.P., folio 60, James G. M. Glass, D.D., "Brief Sketch of the Life of George Rainsford Fairbanks, M.A., LL.D.," typescript, n.d., 7 pp.

40. An account of the initial meeting and first organization of the society is given in Watt Marchman, "The Florida Historical Society, 1856–1861, 1879, 1902–1940," *Florida Historical Quarterly* (July 1940), pp. 6–9.

41. *The Early History of Florida: An Introductory Lecture Deliv-*

ered before the Florida Historical Society, April 15, 1857, with an Appendix Containing the Constitution, Organization, and List of Members of the Society (St. Augustine: Florida Historical Society, 1857), 31 pp. Curiously, the later title, "Florida Historical Society," is used here instead of the name officially designated at that time, "The Historical Society of Florida." The lecture alone, without appendix, was later published under the title "Romantic History of Florida" in *DeBow's Review* 24 (March, April, May 1858): 245-50, 274-77, 372-82. Copies of both printings of the lecture are in the collection of the St. Augustine Historical Society.

42. Ibid., p. 22.

43. Ibid., p. 24.

44. The best existing account of Smith's life is given by Alexander J. Wall, director of the New York Historical Society, in an unpublished manuscript "Buckingham Smith, 1810-1871," 21 pp., in the St. Augustine Historical Society Library. The date of the manuscript is probably 1941, the date when Wall, representing the New York Historical Society, placed a memorial tablet upon the grave of Smith in the Huguenot Cemetery in St. Augustine. A copy of the manuscript is found in the P. K. Yonge Library of Florida History, University of Florida. It is the basis of the short account of Smith's life given in Ray E. Held, "Spanish Florida in American Historiography, 1821-1921" (Ph.D. dissertation, University of Florida, 1955), pp. 149-63.

45. Held, "Florida Historiography," p. 151*n*.

46. Smith to E. G. Squier, 1853, quoted in Wall, "Buckingham Smith," p. 14.

47. Of the Archivo de Las Indias at Seville, Smith wrote in 1856: "There are riches for us at Sevilla enough for our utmost indulgence, could I be there permanently—I have the force of the government with me, but it can do no more, I am persuaded. It is only once or twice in a man's lifetime that the wave comes that can take him on and I am now upon it, but crippled by the narrowness of my means and the requirement of the government keeps me on less than sussistence and does not allow me to have the capital." Quoted in Wall, "Buckingham Smith," p. 16.

48. Smith, *Colección de varios documentos para la historia de la Florida y tierras adyacentes* . . . vol. 1 (London: Trübner y compañia, 1857), 208 pp. The actual printing of this work was done in Spain, despite the London imprint.

49. "Título de adelantado de la Florida, expedido á favor de Pero Mendez de Avilés," ibid., pp. 13-15.

50. "Testamento de Pedro Menéndez de Avilés, sobrino y heredero

del Adelantado de la Florida del mismo nombre, otorgado en Valladolid á 18 de Diciembre de 1618," ibid., pp. 19–25.

51. "Oficio de D. Lucas de Palazio, gobernador de San Agustín, al Exmo. Señor D. Julian de Arriaga, en que manifiesta el mal estado de la guarnición del presidio y remite un estado de la fuerza, el qual se inserta á continuación," ibid., pp. 28–29.

52. "Memoria de Juan de la Vandera, en que se hace relación de los lugares y tierra de la Florida por donde el Capitan Juan Pardo entró á dexubrir camino para Nueva España por los años de 1566, 1567," ibid., pp. 15–19.

53. F.P., folio 63, Smith to Fairbanks, Madrid, March 10, 1858; Madrid, April 7, 1858. In the first communication Smith expressed his pleasure that the engravings he had sent Fairbanks had arrived safely. He went on to state his intention, "if I ever utter another vol[ume] to produce Phil[ip] II who was very much gratified with the conduct of his Admiral [Menéndez] in Florida in his treatment of the French. . . . I have just read a letter . . . about the papers of the Franciscans supposed to be in Havana. . . . *We must get those papers*, and have them in Augustine for the Society. . . . I tell you we know *very* little of the history of Florida yet." In the second letter Smith referred again to the engravings and said, I "am sure that some of them are pure fancy, others unquestionably came from original paintings." Apparently, the only two engravings sent by Smith which Fairbanks used in this book were those of Fort Caroline and Pedro Menéndez.

54. See F.P., folio 69. The engraving of the Menéndez portrait was done by Franco de Paula Marte in 1791 from a drawing by Josef Camarón, which in turn, apparently, was done from a portrait of Menéndez now in the possession of his descendant, the Conde de Revilla Gigedo, of Avilés and Gijón.

55. See Fairbanks' dedication and p. 6, *infra*.

56. Smith described his unhappy relationship with Dodge in a lengthy letter to the historian Peter Force, dated Valencia, Spain, January 12, 1859, and quoted in Wall, "Buckingham Smith," from which the following critical passages might be excerpted: "Conceited, arrogant, ignorant and big-fisted, his indoor behavior has been the most pitiful. For two years and a half he did his best to make me strike him, or challenge him, I do not know which, and finally told me that he had *done his best to get a fight out of me.* The man has been a little short of crazy with jealousy of me, and that has appeared to be in every sort of thing. I have been cussed & charged with all sorts of dirty acts, and I have been watched as an overseer looks after a vicious slave. . . . He is a *monstrous* fool. . . . My investigations are

over, printing stopped, the documents I sought to get for a wide circle
of our history will never be what I have projected, and all this for the
envy of one poor fool!" Smith is described as having been a large
portly man, somewhat overbearing in manner, and it is difficult to
imagine his being bullied by another.

57. See copy of "Will of Buckingham Smith" in Peck-Burt collection, Old Spanish Treasury, St. Augustine; and a typescript of it in
the St. Augustine Historical Society collection.

58. Smith, trans., *Relation of Alvar Nuñez Cabeça de Vaca* (Al-
bany, N.Y.: J. Munsell for H. C. Murphy, 1871), pp. 255–63. This is
the most reliable bibliography for Smith and one discovers from it
that, if Smith was able to bring out only one collection of transcripts
of Spanish documents during his lifetime, he was successful in bring-
ing out numerous other volumes, mostly translations of chronicles,
relations, and memorials. There are comments on Smith's published
works in Held, "Florida Historiography," pp. 153–64. Microfilm copies
of the Smith transcripts willed to the New York Historical Society
are in the P. K. Yonge Library of Florida History, University of Florida.

59. "Will of Buckingham Smith."

60. Ibid.

61. Madrid, 1723. A full translation was published in 1951: Anthony
Kerrigan, trans., *Barcia's Chronological History of the Continent of
Florida* (Gainesville: University of Florida Press, 1951), 426 pp.

62. Barcia, *Ensayo Cronológico*, pp. 66–140. Like Fairbanks' extracts from Barcia, Barcia himself quoted Solís de Merás at length.
These extracts were the first publication of the Solís de Merás material, which was not published in its entirety until 1893, by E. Ruidíaz y Caravia, *La Florida: su Conquista y Colonización por Pedro
Menéndez de Avilés* (Madrid), vol. 2. What appears to be the original manuscript was discovered by the writer of this introduction in
the possession of the Conde de Revilla Gigedo in Gijón, Spain, and
microfilmed, under which form it can be found today in the Mission
Nombre de Dios Library, St. Augustine, and in the P. K. Yonge Library of Florida History, University of Florida.

63. "Memoria del buen suçesso y buen Viaje que dios nͬo señor
fue servido de dar a la armada que salio de la çiudad de caliz para la
prouinçia y costa de la florida de la qual fue por general el Illustre
señor pero menendez de auiles comendador de la orden de sãtiago."
The first publication in Spanish of this "Memorial" was in the 42-
volume collection of Spanish American documents published in Madrid between 1864 and 1884, *Colleción de documentos inéditos rela-
tivos al descubrimiento, conquista y organización de las antiguas po-*

sesiones españolas de América y Oceanía, 3: 441–79; see Lyle N. McAlister, who was the first to bring this fact to the attention of Florida historians, in his introduction to the facsimile edition of Jeannette Thurber Connor, trans., *Pedro Menéndez de Avilés, Memorial by Gonzalo Solís de Merás* (Gainesville: University of Florida Press, 1964), p. 12 and n. 25. The Spanish text is more readily available today in Eugenio Ruidíaz y Carravia, *La Florida: su Conquista y Colonización por Pedro Menéndez de Avilés* (Madrid, 1893), 2: 431–65. The first full translation into English appeared in Benjamin F. French, *Historical Collections of Louisiana and Florida* (New York: Albert Mason, 1875), pp. 191–234. French was not as careful in his translation as was Fairbanks, as appears from a comparison of their two texts with the original Spanish as published in Ruidíaz. In Fairbanks, p. 23, lines 10–15 (beginning "and if our vessels . . ." and ending ("to preserve them.") are a faithful translation of the text as found in Ruidíaz, p. 453, but are missing entirely from the Benjamin F. French translation!

64. *Recueil de pièces sur la Floride*, inédit. (Paris: A. Vertrand, 1841), pp. 165–232. This is volume 20 of a series of collections of voyages published by Ternaux-Compans in Paris between 1837 and 1841.

65. The East Florida Papers constitute the archives of the Spanish government of East Florida between 1783, when England retroceded the area to Spain, and 1821, when the United States took possession. East Florida was the name given during most of this period to the entire peninsula. Numbering 65,000 documents, the collection was removed to Tallahassee by federal officials in 1869, and thence to the Library of Congress in 1905, where they still remain. The papers were microfilmed by the Mission Nombre de Dios in 1965. A description of their contents is given in Michael V. Gannon, "Mission of Nombre de Dios Library," *The Catholic Historical Review* (October 1965), pp. 376–77. The Montiano correspondence is the only part of the collection that dates from the first Spanish period. Fairbanks' use of the papers can be found in this present volume, pp. 142–52.

66. Nicolas le Challeux, *Discours de l'histoire de la Floride* (Dieppe, 1566); the narrative can be found in Ternaux-Compans, *La Floride*, pp. 247–300.

67. Jacques le Moyne de Morgues, "Brevis Narratio eorum quae in Florida Americae provincia Gallis acciderunt . . ." published in Theodor de Bry, *Collectiones Peregrinationum in Indiam Orientalem et Indiam Occidentalem* (Frankfurt, 1591).

68. The narratives of René Goulaine de Laudonnière, "L'histoire notable de la Floride . . . contenant les trois voyages fait en icelle par certains capitaines et pilotes françois descrit par le capitaine Lau-

donnière . . . à laquelle a esté adjousté un quatriesme voyage fait par le capitaine Gourgues," was available to Fairbanks in English translation, published by Richard Hakluyt in *The Principal Navigations, Voiages, Traffiques, and Discoueries of the English Nation*, 3 vols. (London, 1598–1600).

69. "La reprinse de la Floride par le capitaine Gourgues," in Ternaux-Compans, *La Floride*, pp. 301–65.

70. Bartholomew Rivers Carroll, *Historical Collections of South Carolina . . . from Its First Discovery to Its Independence in the Year 1776*, 2 vols. (New York: Harper & Brothers, 1836).

71. William James Rivers, *A Sketch of the History of South Carolina to . . . 1719 . . .* (Charleston: McCarter & Co., 1856).

72. William Gilmore Simms, *The History of South Carolina, from Its First European Discovery . . . to the Present Time* (Charleston: S. Babcock & Co., 1840).

73. William Roberts, *An Account of the First Discovery and Natural History of Florida . . .* (London: T. Jeffreys, 1763).

74. William Bartram, *Travels through North & South Carolina, Georgia, East & West Florida . . .* (Philadelphia: James & Johnson, 1791).

75. William Stork, *An Account of East Florida, with a Journal Kept by John Bartram of Philadelphia . . .* (London: W. Nicholl, 1766).

76. Bernard Romans, *A Concise Natural History of East and West Florida . . .* (New York: R. Aitken, 1775); same, facsimile edition (Gainesville: University of Florida Press, 1962).

77. See Louis De Vorsey, Jr., ed., *Reprint of the General Survey in the Southern District of North America*, by William Gerard De Brahm (Columbia: University of South Carolina Press, 1971).

78. John Lee Williams, *The Territory of Florida . . . from the First Discovery to the Present Time* (New York: A. T. Goodrich, 1837); same, facsimile edition (Gainesville: University of Florida Press, 1962).

79. Anon., *Narrative of a Voyage to the Spanish Main . . . Sketches of the Province of East Florida* (London: John Miller, 1819).

80. William Cullen Bryant, *Letters of a Traveller; or, Notes of Things Seen in Europe and America* (New York: George P. Putnam, 1850).

81. Reliable accounts in the English language of Florida's colonial history, and St. Augustine's in particular, were nonexistent at the time Fairbanks wrote. The generation immediately preceding Fairbanks had to rely on brief historical sketches that were generally descriptive in character and repeated many errors of fact. One may name, in this connection: William Darby, *Memoir on the Geography*

and Natural and Civil History of Florida (Philadelphia: T. H. Palmer,
1821); James Grant Forbes, *Sketches, Historical and Topographical,
of the Floridas* (New York: C. S. Van Winkle, 1821); same, facsimile
edition (Gainesville: University of Florida Press, 1964); Charles
Blacker Vignoles, *Observations upon the Floridas* (New York: E. Bliss
& E. White, 1823); John Lee Williams, *Territory of Florida*; and Rufus
King Sewall, *Sketches of St. Augustine, with a View of Its History
and Advantages as a Resort for Invalids* (New York: George P. Putnam, 1848). Williams' work was the first to make any use at all of
Spanish records. Sewall's work, by a Presbyterian minister from Philadelphia, was the first to concentrate on St. Augustine alone. Sewall
was writing more a description for visitors than a history of the town,
and it appears that the 30-page historical review that he gave of St.
Augustine was based primarily upon that of Williams. Most extant
copies of the work are found with pages 39 and 40 ripped from the
binding. On those pages Sewall referred to the Minorcan population
of St. Augustine as being "of servile extraction," and added: "They
lack enterprise. Most of them are without education." When the
book appeared in St. Augustine, on October 21, 1848, the pages containing these derogatory sentences were ripped from almost every
copy before sale was permitted. When the author, who was in town,
protested, a mob of Minorcans gathered in front of his house and
threatened to do him personal injury. Sewall managed to engineer
his escape with the help of a band of Protestant "Anglo-American
citizens" who exchanged blows with the Minorcans in the street. A
few injuries and minor property damage resulted.

82. *Introductory Lecture*, p. 19.

83. Connor, *Menéndez de Avilés*, p. 123.

84. Contemporary historians tend to emphasize Menéndez' tacti-
cal situation: (1) the large number of French who, greatly outnumber-
ing his own forces, could not safely be guarded with the weapons
available at that time; (2) the scarcity of provisions, particularly food,
which made it difficult to care for his own colony (many of whom
would die from starvation and disease before the end of January
1566) and probably impossible to assume the burden of care for a
large number of captives; and (3) the absence of ship transports with
which to send his prisoners away. Some recent interpretations of these
events conclude that Menéndez' words to the Frenchmen contained
implied assurances of mercy; other stress the fact that the perpetual
state of war between Spain and France in North America, even while
peace reigned in Europe, explained in great part Menéndez' actions.
See Woodbury Lowery, *The Spanish Settlements within the Present
Limits of the United States: Florida, 1562–1574* (New York: G. P.

Putnam's Sons, 1905), pp. 205-6, 421-25; Edward Gaylord Bourne, *Spain in America* (New York: Harper & Brothers, 1906), p. 186; Herbert Eugene Bolton, *The Spanish Borderlands: A Chronicle of Old Florida and the Southwest* (New Haven: Yale University Press, 1921), pp. 149-50; Jeannette Thurber Connor, *Menéndez de Avilés*, p. 38; Henry Folmer, *Franco-Spanish Rivalry in North America, 1524-1763* (Glendale, Calif.: Arthur H. Clark Co., 1953), p. 100; Albert Manucy, *Florida's Menéndez, Captain General of the Open Sea* (St. Augustine: St. Augustine Historical Society, 1965), p. 96; Charlton W. Tebeau, *A History of Florida* (Coral Gables, Fla.: University of Miami Press, 1971), pp. 35-36.

85. See the introduction by David L. Dowd to Jeannette Thurber Connor, ed., *The Whole and True Discouerye of Terra Florida*, by Jean Ribaut (facsimile edition, Gainesville: University of Florida Press, 1964), pp. xlvii, liii, n. 4.

86. F.P., folio 69, Baker & Godwin, Dr., to Fairbanks, New York City, May 15, 1858.

87. F.P., folio 69, Baker & Godwin to Fairbanks, New York City, July 2, 1860.

88. Jacksonville, Fla.: Columbus Drew, 1868.

89. Ibid., p. 120.

90. Jacksonville, Fla.: Horace Drew, 1881.

91. William Whitwell Dewhurst, *The History of St. Augustine* (New York: G. P. Putnam's Sons, 1881); Charles Bingham Reynolds, *Old Saint Augustine: A History of Three Centuries* (St. Augustine: E. H. Reynolds, 1885). In late life Reynolds engaged in correspondence with Fairbanks' son-in-law, James G. Glass, about such matters as the so-called slave market on the east side of the plaza in St. Augustine. Glass advised Reynolds that, "I have heard him [Fairbanks] say on more than one occasion, that no slave had ever been sold from that market"; F.P., folio 73, Glass to Reynolds, Sewanee, Tenn., October 5, 1938. In reply the same year, Reynolds wrote: "I well remember the Fairbanks home out beyond the City gate with its passion-vine flowers; but I do not recollect knowing Major Fairbanks. . . . He was one who had much to do with my interest in Saint Augustine and Florida history; and his inspiration has been lasting. . . . What would he say now to Saint Augustine's degradation by the pseudo historians? . . . In my day the residents of Saint Augustine were of a different type. They would never have thought of bamboozling the stranger within the gates"; F.P., folio 73, Reynolds to Glass, Mountain Lake, N.J., November 7, 1938.

92. Philadelphia: J. B. Lippincott & Co.; Jacksonville, Fla.: Columbus Drew, 1871, 350 pp. The year 1512 was yet again erroneously given as the date of Ponce de León's discovery.

93. *Florida, Its History and Its Romance: The Oldest Settlement in the United States, Associated with the Most Romantic Events of American History under the Spanish, French, English, and American Flags, 1497-1904* (Jacksonville, Fla.: H. & W. B. Drew Co., 1904), xiii, 311 pp.

94. There is a considerable body of correspondence and other material from the Civil War period in the Fairbanks papers, folios 1, 10, 26, 30, 32, 37, 40, 54, and 71. Fairbanks' connections with the University of the South have been described by himself in *History of the University of the South* (Jacksonville, Fla.: H. & W. B. Drew Co., 1905); by Arthur Benjamin Chitty, Jr., *Reconstruction at Sewanee: The Founding of the University of the South and Its First Administration, 1857-1872* (Sewanee, Tenn.: The University Press, 1954); and by John Bell Henneman and William Porcher DuBose, "George Rainsford Fairbanks, 1820-1906, latest surviving member of the original board of trustees of the University of the South," *The Sewanee Review* (October 1906), pp. 3-13.

95. DuBose, ibid., p. 13.

Geo. R. Fairbanks.

From the edition of 1881.

PUBLIC SQUARE, St AUGUSTINE.

THE

HISTORY AND ANTIQUITIES

OF THE CITY OF

ST. AUGUSTINE, FLORIDA

FOUNDED A. D. 1565.

COMPRISING

SOME OF THE MOST INTERESTING PORTIONS

OF THE

EARLY HISTORY OF FLORIDA.

BY

GEORGE R. FAIRBANKS,
VICE-PRESIDENT OF THE FLORIDA HISTORICAL SOCIETY.

NEW YORK:

CHARLES B. NORTON;

AGENT FOR LIBRARIES.

1858.

BAKER & GODWIN, Printers,
1 Spruce St., N. Y.

RESPECTFULLY INSCRIBED

TO

BUCKINGHAM SMITH, ESQ.,

U. S. SECRETARY OF LEGATION AT MADRID,

TO WHOSE EFFORTS IN THE

DISCOVERY AND PRESERVATION OF THE HISTORY AND ANTIQUITIES

OF THE SPANISH DOMINION IN AMERICA,

A GRATEFUL ACKNOWLEDGMENT

IS DUE FROM

American Scholars.

PREFACE.

———•◆•———

This volume, relating to the history and antiquities of the oldest settlement in the United States, has grown out of a lecture delivered by the author, and which he was desired to embody in a more permanent form.

The large amount of interesting material in my possession, has made my work rather one of laborious condensation than expansion.

I have endeavored to preserve as fully as possible, the style and quaintness of the old writers from whom I have drawn, rather than to transform or embellish the narrative with the supposed graces of modern diction; and, as much of the work consisted in translations from foreign idioms, this peculiarly un-English style, if I may so call it, will be more noticeably observed. I have mainly sought

to give it a permanent value, as founded on the most
reliable ancient authorities; and thus, to the extent
of the ground which it covers, to make it a valuable
addition to the history of our country.

In that portion of the work devoted to the
destruction of the Huguenot colony and the forces
of Ribault, I have in the main, followed the Spanish
accounts, desiring to divest the narrative of all
suspicion of prejudice or unfairness; *Barcia*, the
principal authority, as is well known, professing the
same faith as Menendez, and studiously endeavoring
throughout his work, to exalt the character of the
Adelantado.

I am under great obligations to my friend, BUCK-
INGHAM SMITH, ESQ., for repeated favors in the course
of its preparation.

CONTENTS.

ILLUSTRATIONS.

HISTORY AND ANTIQUITIES

OF THE CITY OF

ST. AUGUSTINE, FLORIDA.

CHAPTER I.

INTRODUCTORY.

THE Saint Augustine of the present and the St. Augustine of the past, are in striking contrast.

We see, to-day, a town less in population than hundreds of places of but few months' existence, dilapidated in its appearance, with the stillness of desolation hanging over it, its waters undisturbed except by the passing canoe of the fisherman, its streets unenlivened by busy traffic, and at mid-day it might be supposed to have sunk under the enchanter's wand into an almost eternal sleep.

With no participation in the active schemes of life, and no hopes for the future; with no emulation, and no feverish visions of future greatness; with no corner lots on sale or in demand; with no stocks, save those devoted to disturbers of the public peace; with no excitements and no events; a quiet, undisturbed, dreamy vision of still life surrounds its walls, and creates a sensation of entire repose, pleasant or otherwise, as it falls upon the heart of the weary

2

wanderer sick of life's busy bustle, or upon the restless mind of him who looks to nothing as life except perpetual, unceasing action ; the one rejoicing in its rest, the other chafing under its monotony. And yet, about the old city there clings a host of historic associations, which throw around it a charm which few can fail to feel.

Its life is in its past; and when we recall the fact that it was the first permanent settlement of the white man, by more than forty years, in this confederacy ; that here for the first time, isolated within the shadows of the primeval forest, the civilization of the Old World made its abiding place, where all was new, and wild, and strange ; that this now so insignificant place was the key of an empire ; that upon its fate rested the destiny of a nation ; that its occupation or retention decided the fate of a people ; that it was itself a vice-provincial court, boasted of its adelantados, men of the first mark and note, of its Royal Exchequer, its public functionaries, its brave men at arms ; that its proud name, conferred by its monarch, " *La siempre fiel Ciudad de San Augustin*," —The ever faithful City of St. Augustine,—stood out upon the face of history ; that here the cross was first planted ; that from the Papal throne itself rescripts were addressed to its governors ; that the first great efforts at christianizing the fierce tribes

of America proceeded from this spot; that the martyr's blood was first here shed; that within these
quiet walls the din of arms, the noise of battle, and
the fierce cry of assaulting columns, have been
heard;—Who will not then feel that we stand on
historic ground, and that an interest attaches to the
annals of this ancient city far more than is possessed
by mere brick and mortar, rapid growth, or unwont-
ed prosperity? Moss-grown and shattered, it appeals
to our instinctive feelings of reverence for antiquity;
and we feel desirous to know the history of its
earlier days.

CHAPTER II.

FIRST DISCOVERY, 1512, TO 1565.—JUAN PONCE DE LEON.

AMONG the sturdy adventurers of the sixteenth century who sought both fame and fortune in the path of discovery, was Ponce de Leon, a companion of Columbus on his second voyage, a veteran and bold mariner, who, after a long and adventurous life, feeling the infirmities of age and the shadows of the decline of life hanging over him, willingly credited the tale that in this, the beautiful land of his imagination, there existed a fountain whose waters could restore youth to palsied age, and beauty to efface the marks of time.

The story ran that far to the north there existed a land abounding in gold and in all manner of desirable things, but, above all, possessing a river and springs of so remarkable a virtue that their waters would confer immortal youth on whoever bathed in them ; that upon a time, a considerable expedition of the Indians of Cuba had departed northward, in search of this beautiful country and these waters of immortality, who had never returned, and who, it was supposed, were in a renovated state, still enjoying the felicities of the happy land.

Furthermore, Peter Martyr affirms, in his second decade, addressed to the Pope, "that among the islands on the north side of Hispaniola, there is one about three hundred and twenty-five leagues distant, as they say which have searched the same, in the which is a continual spring of running water, of such marvelous virtue that the water thereof being drunk, perhaps with some diet, maketh old men young again. And here I must make protestation to your Holiness not to think this to be said lightly, or rashly; for they have so spread this rumor for a truth throughout all the court, that not only all the people, but also many of them whom wisdom or fortune hath divided from the common sort, think it to be true." * Thoroughly believing in the verity of this pleasant account, this gallant cavalier fitted out an expedition from Porto Rico, and in the progress of his search came upon the coast of Florida, on Easter Monday, 1512, supposing then, and for a long

---

* The fountain of youth is a very ancient fable; and the reader will be reminded of the amusing story of the accomplishment of this miracle told in Hawthorne's Twice Told Tales, and of the marvelous effects produced by imbibing this celebrated spring water.

period afterwards, that it was an island. Partly in consequence of the bright spring verdure and flowery plains that met his eye, and the magnificence of the magnolia, the bay, and the laurel, and partly in honor of the day, Pascua Florida, or Palm Sunday, and reminded, probably, of its appropriateness by the profusion of the cabbage palms near the point of his landing, he gave to the country the name of Florida.

On the 3d of April, 1512, three hundred and forty-five years ago, he landed a few miles north of St. Augustine, and took possession of the country for the Spanish crown. He found the natives fierce and implacable; and after exploring the country for some distance around, and trying the virtue of all the streams, and growing neither younger nor handsomer, he left the country without making a permanent settlement.

The subsequent explorations of Narvaez, in 1526, and of De Soto, in 1539, were made in another portion of our State, and do not bear immediately upon the subject of our investigation, although forming a most interesting portion of our general history.

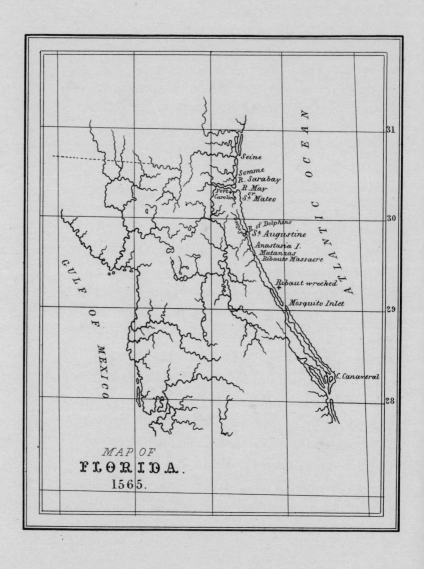

MAP OF
FLORIDA.
1565.

CHAPTER III.

RIBAULT, LAUDONNIERE, AND MENENDEZ—SETTLEMENTS OF
THE HUGUENOTS, AND FOUNDATION OF ST. AUGUSTINE.
1562—1565—1568.

THE settlement of Florida had its origin in the
religious troubles experienced by the Huguenots
under Charles IX. in France.

Their distinguished leader, Admiral Coligny, as
early as 1555 projected colonies in America, and
sent an expedition to Brazil, which proved unsuccessful. Having procured permission from Charles IX.
to found a colony in Florida; a designation which
embraced in rather an indefinite manner the whole
country from the Chesapeake to the Tortugas, he
sent an expedition in 1562 from France, under command of Jean Ribault, composed of many young men
of good family. They first landed at the St. John's
River, where they erected a monument, but finally
established a settlement at Port Royal, South Carolina, and erected a fort. After some months, however, in consequence of dissensions among the officers

of the garrison, and difficulties with the Indians, this settlement was abandoned.

In 1564 another expedition came out under the command of Réné de Laudonnière, and made their first landing at the River of Dolphins, being the present harbor of St. Augustine, and so named by them in consequence of the great number of Dolphins (Porpoises) seen by them at its mouth. They afterwards coasted to the north, and entered the River St. Johns, called by them the River May.

Upon an examination of this river Laudonnière concluded to establish his colony on its banks; and proceeding about two leagues above its month, built a fort upon a pleasant hill of "mean height" which, in honor of his sovereign, he named Fort Caroline.

The colonists after a few months were reduced to great distress, and were about taking measures to abandon the country a second time, when Ribault arrived with reinforcements.

It is supposed that intelligence of these expeditions was communicated by the enemies of Coligny to the court of Spain.

Jealousy of the aggrandizement of the French in the New World, mortification for their own unsuccessful efforts in that quarter, and a still stronger motive of hatred to the faith of the Huguenot, induced the bigoted Philip II. of Spain, to dispatch

Pedro Menendez de Aviles, a brave, bigoted, and remorseless soldier, to drive out the French colony, and take possession of the country for himself.

The compact made between the king and Menendez was, that he should furnish one galleon completely equipped, and provisions for a force of six hundred men; that he should conquer and settle the country. He obligated himself to carry one hundred horses, two hundred horned cattle, four hundred hogs, four hundred sheep and some goats, and *five hundred slaves* (for which he had a permission free of duties), the third part of which should be men, for his own service and that of those who went with him, to aid in cultivating the land and building. That he should take twelve priests, and four fathers of the Jesuit order. He was to build two or three towns of one hundred families, and in each town should build a fort according to the nature of the country. He was to have the title of Adelantado of the country, as also to be entitled a Marquis and his heirs after him, to have a tract of land, receive a salary of 2000 ducats, a percentage of the royal duties, and have the freedom of all the other ports of New Spain.*

His force consisted, at starting, of eleven sail of

---

* Barcia Ensayo, Cron. 66.

vessels with two thousand and six hundred men; but, owing to storms and accidents, not more than one half arrived. He came upon the coast on the 28th August, 1565, shortly after the arrival of the fleet of Ribault. On the 7th day of September Menendez cast anchor in the River of Dolphins, the harbor of St. Augustine. He had previously discovered and given chase to some of the vessels of Ribault, off the mouth of the River May. The Indian village of Selooe then stood upon the site of St. Augustine, and the landing of Menendez was upon the spot where the city of St. Augustine now stands.

Fray Francisco Lopez de Mendoza, the Chaplain of the Expedition, thus chronicles the disembarkation and attendant ceremonies :—

" On Saturday the 8th day of September, the day of the nativity of our Lady, the General disembarked, with numerous banners displayed, trumpets and other martial music resounding, and amid salvos of artillery.

"Carrying a cross, I proceeded at the head, chanting the hymn *Te Deum Laudamus*. The General marched straight up to the cross, together with all those who accompanied him ; and, kneeling, they all kissed the cross. A great number of Indians looked upon these ceremonies, and imitated whatever they saw done. Thereupon the General took possession of the country in the name of his Majesty. All the officers then took an oath of allegiance to him, as their general and as adelantado of the whole country."

The name of St. Augustine was given, in the usual manner of the early voyagers, because they had arrived upon the coast on the day dedicated in their calendar to that eminent saint of the primitive church, revered alike by the good of all ages for his learning and piety.

The first troops who landed, says Mendoza, were well received by the Indians, who gave them a large mansion belonging to the chief, situated near the banks of the river. The engineer officers immediately erected an entrenchment of earth, and a ditch around this house, with a slope made of earth and fascines, these being the only means of defense which the country presents; for, says the father with surprise, "there is not a stone to be found in the whole country." They landed eighty cannon from the ships, of which the lightest weighed two thousand five hundred pounds.

But in the mean time Menendez had by no means forgotten the errand upon which he principally came; and by inquiries of the Indians he soon learned the position of the French fort and the condition of its defenders. Impelled by necessity, Laudonnière had been forced to seize from the Indians food to support his famished garrison, and had thus incurred their enmity, which was soon to produce its sad results.

The Spaniards numbered about six hundred combatants, and the French about the same; but arrangements had been made for further accessions to the Spanish force, to be drawn from St. Domingo and Havana, and these were daily expected.

It was the habit of those days, to devolve almost every event upon the ordering of a special providence; and each nation had come to look upon itself almost in the light of a peculiar people, led like the Israelites of old by signs and wonders; and as in their own view all their actions were directed by the design of advancing God's glory as well as their own purposes, so the blessing of Heaven would surely accompany them in all their undertakings.

So believed the crusaders on the plains of Palestine ; so believed the conquerors of Mexico and Peru ; so believed the Puritan settlers of New England (alike in their Indian wars and their oppressive social polity) ; and so believed, also, the followers of Menendez and of Ribault; and in this simple and trusting faith, the worthy chaplain gives us the following account of the miraculous escape and deliverance of a portion of the Spanish fleet :—

"God and his Holy Mother have performed another great miracle in our favor. The day following the landing of the General in the fort, he said to us that he was very uneasy, because· his galley and another vessel were at anchor, isolated and a league at sea, being unable to enter the port on account of the shallowness of the water, and that he feared that the French might come and capture or maltreat them. As soon as this idea came to him he departed, with fifty men, to go on board of his galleon. He gave orders to three shallops which were moored in the river to go out and take on board the provisions and troops which were on board the galleon. The next day, a shallop having gone out thither, they took on board as much of the provisions as they could, and more than a hundred men who were in the vessel, and returned towards the shore; but half a league before arriving at the bar they were overtaken by so complete a calm that they were unable to proceed further, and thereupon cast anchor and passed the night in that place. The day following at break of day they raised anchor as ordered by the pilot, as the rising of the tide began to be felt. When it was fully light they saw astern of them at the poop of the vessel, two French ships which during the night had been in search of

them. The enemy arrived with the intention of
making an attack upon us. The French made all
haste in their movements, for we had no arms on
board, and·had only embarked the provisions. When
day appeared, and our people discovered the French,
they addressed their prayers to our Lady of *Bon
Secours d' Utrera*, and supplicated her to grant them
a little wind, for the French were already close up
to them. They say that *Our Lady* descended, her-
self, upon the vessel; for the wind freshened and
blew fair for the bar, so that the shallop could enter
it. The French followed it; but as the bar has but
little depth and their vessels were large, they were
not able to go over it, so that our men and the provisions made a safe harbor. When it became still
clearer they perceived besides the two vessels of the
enemy, four others at a distance, being the same
which we had seen in port the evening of our arrival. They were well furnished with both troops
and artillery, and had directed themselves for our
galleon and the other ship, which were alone at sea.
In this circumstance God accorded us two favors:
the first was, that the same evening after they had
discharged the provisions and the troops I have
spoken of, at midnight the galleon and other vessel
put to sea without being perceived by the enemy;
the one for Spain, and the other for Havana for the

purpose of seeking the fleet which was there; and in this way neither was taken.

"The second favor, by which God rendered us a still greater service, was that on the day following the one I have described there arose a storm, and so great a tempest that certainly the greater part of the French vessels must have been lost at sea; for they were overtaken upon the most dangerous coast I have ever seen, and were very close to the shore; and if our vessels, that is, the galleon and its consort, are not shipwrecked, it is because they were already more than twelve leagues off the coast, which gave them the facility of running before the wind, and maneuvering as well as they could, relying upon the aid of God to preserve them." *

Menendez had ascertained from the Indians that a large number of the French troops had embarked on board of the vessels which he had seen off the

---

* The Galleon spoken of was Menendez's own flag-ship, the El Pelayo, the largest vessel in his fleet, fitted out at his own expense, and which had brought four hundred men. He had put on board of her a lieutenant and some soldiers, besides fifteen Lutherans as prisoners, whom he was sending home to the Inquisition at Seville. The orders to his officers were to go as speedily as possible to the island of Hispaniola, to bring provisions and additional forces. Upon the passage, the Lutheran prisoners, with some Levantine sailors, rose upon the Spaniards, killed the commander, and carried the vessel into Denmark. Menendez was much chagrined when he ascertained the fate of his favorite galleon, a long period afterwards.

harbor, and he had good ground for believing that these vessels would either be cast helpless upon the shore, or be driven off by the tempest to such a distance as would render their return for some days impossible. He at once conceived the project of attacking the French fort upon the river May, by land.

A council of war was held, and after some discussion, for the most part adverse to the plan proposed by him, Menendez spoke as follows :—" Gentlemen and Brothers ! we have before us now an opportunity which if improved by us will have a happy result. I am satisfied that the French fleet which four days since fled from me, and has now come to seek me, has been reinforced with the larger part of the garrison of their fort, to which, nor to port, will they be able to return for many days according to appearances ; and since they are all Lutherans, as we learned before we sailed from Spain, by the edicts which Jean Ribault published before embarking, in order that no Catholic at the peril of his life should go in his fleet, nor any Catholic books be taken ; and this they themselves declared to us the night they fled from us, and hence our war must be to blood and fire, not only on account of the orders we are under, but because they have sought us in order to destroy us, that we should not plant our holy religion in these regions, and to establish their own abominable and crazy sect among the Indians; so that the more promptly we shall punish them, we shall the more speedily do a service to our God and our king, and comply with our conscience and our duty.

"To accomplish this, we must choose five hundred arquebuse men and pikemen, and carry provisions in our knapsacks for eight days, divided into ten companies, each one with its standard and its captain, and go with this force by land to examine the settlements and fort of our enemies; and as no one knows the road, I will guide you within two points by a mariner's compass; and where we cannot get along, we will open a way with our axes; and moreover, I have with me a Frenchman who has been more than a year at their fort, and who says he knows the ground for two leagues around the fort.

"If we shall arrive without discovery, it may be that falling upon it at daylight we may take it, by planting upon it twenty scaling ladders, at the cost of fifty lives. If we are discovered, we can form in the shelter of the wood, which I am assured is not more than a quarter of a league distant, and planting there ten standards, send forward a trumpeter requiring them to leave the fort and the country, and return to their own country, offering them ships

3

and provisions for the voyage. They will imagine that we have a much greater army with us, and they may surrender; and if they do not, we shall at least accomplish that they will leave us undisturbed in this our own settlement, and we shall know the way, so that we may return to destroy them the succeeding spring."

After some discussion, it was concluded that after hearing mass, they should undertake the expedition on the third day. Considerable opposition was manifested on the part of the officers; but, with a consummate knowledge of human nature, the adelantado got up the most splendid dinner in his power, and invited his recreant officers to the repast, and dexterously appealed to their fears, as well as their pride, and overcame their reluctance to undertake the unknown dangers of a first march through Florida at a wet season, an actual acquaintance with which would still more have dampened their ardor.

The troops assembled promptly upon the day appointed, at the sound of the trumpet, the fife and the drum, and they all went to hear mass, except Juan de Vicente, who said he had a disorder of the stomach, and in his leg; and when some friends wished to urge his coming, he replied,—" I vow to God, that I will wait until the news comes that our force is entirely cut off, when we who remain will

embark in our three vessels, and go to the Indies,
where there will be no necessity of our all perishing
like beasts."

This Juan Vicente seems to have been an apt
specimen of a class of croakers not peculiar to any
age or country. Of his further history, the chronicle
gives other instances of a similar spirit; and his sole
claim to immortality, like that of many an other, is
founded upon his impudence.

CHAPTER IV.

THE ATTACK ON FORT CAROLINE.—1565.

THE troops, having heard mass, marched out in order, preceded by twenty Biscayans and Asturians having as their captain Martin de Ochoa, a leader of great fidelity and bravery, furnished with axes to open a road where they could not get along. At this moment there arrived two Indians, who said that they had been at the French fort six days before, and who "seemed like angels" to the soldiers, sent to guide their march. Halting for refreshment and rest wherever suitable places could be found, and the Adelantado always with the vanguard, in four days they reached the vicinity of the fort, and came up within less than a quarter of a league of it, concealed by a grove of pine trees. It rained heavily, and a severe storm prevailed. The place where they had halted was a very bad one, and very marshy ; but he decided to stop there, and went back to seek the rearguard, lest they might lose the way.

FORT CAROLINE.

Erected 1564

About ten at night the last of the troops arrived, very wet indeed, for there had been much rain during the four days; they had passed marshes with the water rising to their waists, and every night there was so great a flood that they were in great danger of losing their powder, their match-fire, and their biscuit; and they became desperate, cursing those who had brought them there, and themselves for coming.

Menendez pretended not to hear their complaints, not daring to call a council as to proceeding or returning, for both officers and soldiers went forward very inquietly. Remaining firm in his own resolve, two hours before dawn he called together the Master of the Camp and the Captains, to whom he said that during the whole night he had sought of God and his most Holy Mother, that they would favor him and instruct him what he should do, most advantageous for their holy service; and he was persuaded that they had all done the same. " But now, Gentlemen," he proceeded, " we must make some determination, finding ourselves exhausted, lost, without ammunition or provisions, and without the hope of relief."

Some answered very promptly, " Why should they waste their time in giving reasons ? for, unless they returned quickly to St. Augustine, they would be reduced to eating palmettos;* and the longer they delayed, the greater trouble they would have."

The Adelantado said to them that what they said seemed very reasonable, but he would ask of them to hear some reasons to the contrary, without being offended. He then proceeded—after having smoothed down their somewhat ruffled dispositions, considerably disturbed by their first experience in encountering the hardships of such a march—to show them that the danger of retreat was then greater than an advance would be, as they would lose alike the respect of their friends and foes. That if, on the contrary, they attacked the fort, whether they succeeded in taking it or not, they would gain honor and reputation.

Stimulated by the speech of their General, they demanded to be led to the attack, and the arrangements for the assault were at once made. Their French prisoner was placed in the advance; but the darkness of the night and the severity of the storm rendered it impossible to proceed, and they halted in a marsh, with the water up to their knees, to await daylight.

At dawn, the Frenchman recognized the country,

---

* A low palm, bearing an oily berry.

and the place where they were, and where stood the
fort; upon which the Adelantado ordered them to
march, enjoining upon all, at the peril of their lives,
to follow him; and coming to a small hill, the
Frenchman said that behind that stood the fort,
about three bow-shots distant, but lower down, near
the river. The General put the Frenchman into the
custody of Castaneda. He went up a little higher,
and saw the river and one of the houses, but he was
not able to discover the fort, although it was adjoining them; and he returned to Castaneda, with
whom now stood the Master of the Camp and Ochoa,
and said to them that he wished to go lower down,
near to the houses which stood behind the hill, to
see the fortress and the garrison, for, as the sun was
now up, they could not attack the fort without a
reconnoisance. This the Master of the Camp would
not permit him to do, saying this duty appertained
to him; and he went alone with Ochoa near to the
houses, from whence they discovered the fort; and
returning with their information, they came to two
paths, and leaving the one by which they came, they
took the other. The Master of the Camp discovered
his error, coming to a fallen tree, and turned his
face to inform Ochoa, who was following him; and
as they turned to seek the right path, he stopped in
advance, and the sentinel discovered them, who

imagined them to be French; but examining them
he perceived they were unknown to him. He hailed,
"Who goes there?" Ochoa answered, "Frenchmen." The sentinel was confirmed in his supposition
that they were his own people, and approached
them; Ochoa did the same; but seeing they were
not French, the sentinel retreated. Ochoa closed
with him, and with his drawn sword gave him a cut
over the head, but did not hurt him much, as the
sentinel fended off the blow with his sword; and the
Master of the Camp coming up at this moment, gave
him a thrust, from which he fell backwards, making
a loud outcry. The Master of the Camp, putting
his sword to his breast, threatened him with instant
death unless he kept silence. They tied him thereupon, and took him to the General, who, hearing the
noise, thought the Master of the Camp was being
killed, and meeting with the Sergeant-major, Francisco de Recalde, Diego de Maya, and Andres Lopez
Patino, with their standards and soldiers, without
being able to restrain himself, he cried out, "Santiago! Upon them! Help of God, Victory! The
French are destroyed. The Master of the Camp is
in their fort, and has taken it." Upon which, all
rushed forward in the path without order, the
General remaining behind, repeating what he had
said many times; himself believing it to be certain

that the Master of Camp had taken with him a con-siderable force, and had captured the fort.

So great was the joy of the soldiers, and such their speed, that they soon came up with the Master of the Camp and Ochoa, who was hastening to receive the reward of carrying the good news to the General of the capture of the sentinel. But the Master of the Camp, seeing the spirit which animated the sol-diery, killed the sentinel, and cried out with a loud voice to those who were pressing forward, " Com-rades ! do as I do. God is with us ;" and turned, running towards the fort, and meeting two French-men on the way, he killed one of them, and Andres Lopez Patino the other. Those in the environs of the fort, seeing this tragedy enacted, set up loud outcries ; and in order to know the cause of the alarm, one of the French within opened the postern of the principal gate, which he had no sooner done than it was observed by the Master of the Camp ; and throwing himself upon him, he killed him, and entered the gate, followed by the most active of his followers.

The French awakened by the clamor, some dressed, others in their night-clothes, rushed to the doors of their houses to see what had happened; but they were all killed, except sixty of the more wary, who escaped by leaping the walls.

Immediately the standards of the Sergeant Major and of Diego Mayo were brought in, and set up by Rodrigo Troche and Pedro Valdes Herrera, with two cavaliers, at the same moment. These being hoisted, the trumpets proclaimed the victory, and the bands of soldiers who had entered opened the gates and sought the quarters, leaving no Frenchman alive.

The Adelantado hearing the cries, left Castaneda in his place to collect the people who had not come up, who were at least half the force, and went himself to see if they were in any danger. He arrived at the fort running; and as he perceived that the soldiers gave no quarter to any of the French, he shouted, "That at the penalty of their lives, they should neither wound nor kill any woman, cripple, or child under fifteen years of age." By which seventy persons were saved, *the rest were all killed.*

Renato de Laudonnière, the Commander of the fort, escaped, with his servant and some twenty or thirty others, to a vessel lying in the river.

Such is the Spanish chronicle, contained in Barcia, of the capture of Fort Caroline. Its details in the main correspond with the account of Laudonniére, and of Nicolas Challeux, the author of the letter printed at Lyons, in France, under date of August, 1566, by Jean Saugrain. In some important particulars, however, the historians disagree. It has been already seen that Menendez is represented as having given orders to spare all the women, maimed persons, and all children under fifteen years of age. The French relations of the event, on the contrary, allege that an indiscriminate slaughter took place, and that all were massacred without respect to age, sex, or condition; but as this statement is principally made upon the authority of a terrified and flying soldier, it is alike due to the probabilities of the case, and more agreeable to the hopes of humanity, to lessen somewhat the horrors of a scene which has need of all the palliation which can be drawn from the slightest evidences of compassion on the part of that stern and bigoted leader.

The Spanish statement is further confirmed by other writers, who speak of a vessel being dispatched by Menendez subsequently to carry the survivors to Spain.

CHAPTER V.

ESCAPE OF LAUDONNIERE AND OTHERS FROM FORT CAROLINE:
ADVENTURES OF THE FUGITIVES.

THE narratives of this event are found singularly
full, there being no less than three accounts by fugitives from the massacre. The most complete of these
is that of Nicolas de Challeux, a native of Dieppe,
which was published in the following year. I have
largely transcribed from this quaint and curious narrative, not only an account of the fullness of the details, but also for the light it throws upon the habits
of thought and modes of expression of that day,
when so much was exhibited of an external religious
faith, and so many were found who would fight for
their faith when they refused to adhere to its requirements. There are apparent, also, a close study of the
Scriptures, a great familiarity with its language, a
frequent use of its illustrations, and a disposition to
attribute all things, with a reverent piety, to the
direct personal supervision of the Almighty. With
the aid of the map accompanying the succeeding
chapter, it will not be difficult to trace the perilous

route of escape pursued by De Challeux and his companions, over obstacles much magnified by the terror of the moment and want of familiarity with the country :—

"The number of persons in the fort was two hundred and forty, partly of those who had not recovered from sea-sickness, partly of artisans and of women and children left to the care and diligence of Captain Laudonnière, who had no expectation that it was possible that any force could approach by land to attack him. On which account the guards had withdrawn for the purpose of refreshing themselves a little before sunrise, on account of the bad weather which had continued during the whole night, most of our people being at the time in their beds sleeping. The wicket gate open, the Spanish force, having traversed forests, swamps, and rivers, arrived at break of day, Friday, the 20th September, the weather very stormy, and entered the fort without any resistance, and made a horrible satisfaction of the rage and hate they had conceived against our nation. It was then who should best kill the most men, sick and well, women and little children, in such manner that it is impossible to conceive of a massacre which could equal this for its barbarity and cruelty.

"Some of the more active of our people, jumping from their beds, slipped out and escaped to the vessel in the river. I was myself surprised, going to my duty with my clasp-knife in my hand; for upon leaving my cabin, I met the enemy, and saw no other means of escape but turning my back, and making the utmost possible haste to leap over the palisades, for I was closely pursued, step by step, by a pikeman, and one with a partisan; and I do not know how it was, unless by the grace of God, that my strength was redoubled, old man as I am and greyheaded, a thing which at any other time I could not have done, for the rampart was raised eight or nine feet; I then hastened to secrete myself in the woods, and when I was sufficiently near the edge of the wood at the distance of a good bow-shot, I turned towards the fort and rested a little time, finding myself not pursued; and as from this place all the fort, even the inner-court was distinctly visible to me, looking there I saw a horrible butchery of our men taking place, and three standards of our enemies planted upon the ramparts. Having then lost all hope of seeing our men rally, I resigned all my senses to the Lord. Recommending myself to his mercy, grace, and favor, I threw myself into the wood, for it seemed to me that I could find no greater cruelty among the savage beasts, than that of our enemy which I had seen shown towards our people. But the misery and anguish in which I found myself then, straitened and

oppressed, seeing no longer any means of safety upon
the earth, unless by a special grace of our Lord,
transcending any expectation of man, caused me to
utter groans and sobs, and with a voice broken by
distress to thus cry to the Lord :

" 'O God of our fathers and Lord of all mercy! who
hast commanded us to call upon Thee even from the
depths of hell and the shades of death, promising
forthwith thy aid and succor! show me, for the hope
which I have in Thee, what course I ought to take to
come to the termination of this miserable old age,
plunged into the gulf of grief and bitterness ; at least,
cause that, feeling the effect of Thy mercy, and the
confidence which I have conceived in my heart for
Thy promises, they may not be snatched from me
through fear of savage and furious wild beasts on one
hand, and of our and Thy enemies on the other, who
desire the more to injure us for the memory of Thy
name which is invoked by us than for any other cause;
aid me, my God! assist me, for I am so troubled that I
can do nothing more.'   And while I was making this
prayer, traversing the wood, which was very thick
and matted with briars and thorns, beneath the
large trees where there was neither any road nor
path, scarcely had I trailed my way half an hour,
when I heard a noise like men weeping and groan-
ing near me ; and advancing in the name of God, and

in the confidence of His succor, I discovered one of our people, named Sieur de la Blonderie, and a little behind him another, named Maitre Robert, well known to us all, because he had in charge the prayers at the fort. Immediately afterwards we found also the servant of Sieur d' Ully, the nephew of M. Lebreau, Master Jaques Trussé, and many others; and we assembled and talked over our troubles, and deliberated as to what course we could take to save our lives. One of our number, much esteemed as being very learned in the lessons of Holy Scripture, proposed after this manner: 'Brethren, we see to what extremity we are brought; in whatever direction we turn our eyes, we see only barbarism. The heavens, the earth, the sea, the forest, and men,—in brief, nothing favors us. How can we know that if we yield to the mercy of the Spaniards, they will spare us? and if they should kill us, it will be the suffering of but a moment; they are men, and it may be that, their fury appeased, they may receive us upon some terms; and, moreover, what can we do? Would it not be better to fall into the hands of men, than into the jaws of wild beasts, or die of hunger in a strange land?'

"After he had thus spoken, the greater part of our number were of his opinion, and praised his counsel. Notwithstanding, I pointed out the cruel

animosity still unappeased of our enemies, and that
it was not for any human cause of quarrel, that they
had carried out with such fury their enterprise, but
mainly (as would appear by the notice they had
already given us) because we were of those who were
reformed by the preaching of the Gospel; that we
should be cowards to trust in men, rather than in
God, who gives life to his own in the midst of death,
and gives ordinarily his assistance when the hopes of
men entirely fail.

"I also brought to their minds examples from
Scripture, instancing Joseph, Daniel, Elias, and the
other prophets, as well also the apostles, as St. Peter and St. Paul, who were all drawn out of much
affliction, as would appear by means extraordinary
and strange to the reason and judgment of men.
His arm, said I, is not shortened, nor in any wise en-
feebled; his power is always the same. Do you not
recollect, said I, the flight of the Israelites before
Pharaoh? What hope had that people of escaping from the hands of that powerful tyrant? He
had them, as it were, under his heel. Before them
they had the sea, on either side inaccessible mountains.

"What then? He who opened the sea to make
a path for his people, and made it afterwards to
swallow up his enemies, can not he conduct us by

4

the forest places of this strange country? While
thus discoursing, six of the company followed out
the first proposition, and abandoned us to go and
yield themselves up to our enemies, hoping to find
favor before them. But they learned, immediately
and by experience, what folly it is to trust more in
men than in the promises of the Lord. For having
gone out of the wood, as they descended to the fort
they were immediately seized by the Spaniards and
treated in the same fashion as the others had been.
They were at once killed and massacred, and then
drawn to the banks of the river, where the others
killed at the fort lay in heaps. We who remained in
the wood continued to make our way, and drawing
towards the sea, as well as we could judge, and as it
pleased God to conduct our paths and to straiten our
course, we soon arrived at the brow of a mountain
and from there commenced to see the sea, but it was
still at a great distance; and what was worse, the
road we had to take showed itself wonderfully strange
and difficult. In the first place, the mountain from
which it was necessary for us to descend, was of such
height and ruggedness, that it was not possible for a
person descending to stand upright; and we should
never have dared to descend it but for the hope we
had of sustaining ourselves by the branches of the
bushes, which were frequent upon the side of the

mountain, and to save life, not sparing our hands
which we had all gashed up and bloody, and even
the legs and nearly all the body was torn.   But
descending from the mountain, we did not lose our
view of the sea, on account of a small wood which was
upon a little hill opposite to us; and in order to go to
the wood it was requisite that we should traverse a
large meadow, all mud and quagmire, covered with
briars and other kinds of strange plants; for the stalk
was as hard as wood, and the leaves pricked our feet
and our hands until the blood came, and being all the
while in the water up to the middle, which redoubled
our pain and suffering.   The rain came down upon us
in such manner from heaven, that we were during
all that time between two floods; and the further we
advanced the deeper we found the water.

  " And then, thinking that the last period of our
lives had come, we all embraced each other, and
with a common impulse, we commenced to sigh and
cry to the Lord, accusing our sins and recognizing
the weight of his judgments upon us.   ' Alas!
Lord,' said we, ' what are we but poor worms of
the earth ?   Our souls weakened by grief, surrender
themselves into thy hands.   Oh, Father of Mercy
and God of Love, deliver us from this pain of death !
or if thou wilt that in this desert we shall draw our
last breath, assist us so that death, of all things the

most terrible, shall have no advantage over us, but
that we may remain firm and stable in the sense of
thy favor and good-will, which we have too often
experienced in the cause of thy Christ to give way
to the spirit of Satan, the spirit of despair and of dis-
trust; for if we die, we will protest now before thy
Majesty, that we would die unto thee, and that if we
live it may be to recount thy wonders in the midst
of the assembly of thy servants.' Our prayers
concluded, we marched with great difficulty straight
towards the wood, when we came to a great river
which ran in the midst of this meadow; the channel
was sufficiently narrow but very deep, and ran with
great force, as though all the field ran towards the
sea. This was another addition to our anguish, for
there was not one of our men who would dare to
undertake to cross over by swimming. But in this
confusion of our thoughts, as to what manner to pass
over, I bethought myself of the wood which we had
left behind us. After exhorting my comrades to
patience and a continued trust in the Lord, I returned to the wood, and cut a long pole, with the
good-sized clasp-knife which remained in my hand
from the hour the fort was taken; and I returned to
the others, who awaited me in great perplexity.
'Now, then, comrades,' said I, 'let us see if God,
by means of this stick, will not give us some help to

accomplish our path.' Then we laid the pole upon
the water, and each one by turn taking hold of the
end of the pole, carried it by his side to the midst
of the channel, when losing sight of him we pushed
him with sufficient force to the other bank, where
he drew himself out by the canes and other bushes
growing along its borders; and by his example we
passed over, one at a time; but it was not without
great danger, and not without drinking a great deal
of salt water, in such manner that our hearts were
all trembling, and we were as much overcome as
though we had been half drowned. After we had
come to ourselves and we had resumed courage,
moving on all the time towards the wood, which we
had remarked close to the sea, the pole was not
even needed to pass another creek, which gave us
not much less trouble than the first; but, by the
grace of God, we passed it and entered the wood
the same evening, where we passed the night in
great fear and trembling, standing about against the
trees.

" And, as much as we had labored, even had it been
more, we felt no desire to sleep; for what repose
could there be to spirits in such mortal affright?
Near the break of day, we saw a great beast, like a
deer, at fifty paces from us, who had a great head,
eyes flaming, the ears hanging, and the higher parts

elevated. It seemed to us monstrous, because of its gleaming eyes, wondrously large; but it did not come near to do us any harm.

"The day having appeared, we went out of the wood and returned towards the sea, in which we hoped, after God, as the only means of saving our lives; but we were again cast down and troubled, for we saw before us a country of marsh and muddy quagmires, full of water and covered with briars, like that we had passed the previous day. We marched across this salt marsh; and, in the direction we had to take, we perceived among the briars a body of men, whom we at first thought to be enemies, who had gone there to cut us off; but, upon close observation, they seemed in as sad a plight as ourselves, naked and terrified; and we immediately perceived that they were our own people. It was Captain Laudonnière, his servant-maid, Jacques Morgues of Dieppe (the artist), Francis Duval of Rouen, son of him of the iron crown of Rouen, Niguise de la Cratte, Nicholas the carpenter, the Trumpeter of Sieur Laudonnière, and others, who all together made the number of twenty-six men. Upon deliberating as to what we should do, two of our men mounted to the top of one of the tallest trees and discovered from thence one of our vessels, which was that of Captain Maillard, to whom they

gave a signal, that he might know that we were in
want of help. Thereupon he came towards us with
his small vessel, but in order to reach the banks of
the stream, it was necessary for us to traverse the
briars and two other rivers similar to those which
we passed the previous day; in order to accomplish
which, the pole I had cut the day before was both
useful and necessary, and two others which Sr. de
Laudonnière had provided; and we came pretty near
to the vessel, but our hearts failed us from hunger
and fatigue, and we should have remained where we
were unless the sailors had given us a hand, which
aid was very opportune; and they carried us, one
after the other, to the vessel, on board of which we
were all received well and kindly. They gave us
bread and water, and we began afterwards, little by
little, to recover our strength and vigor; which was
a strong reason that we should recognize the goodness of the Lord, who had saved us against all hope
from an infinity of dangers and from death, by
which we had been surrounded and assaulted from
all quarters, to render him forevermore our thanks
and praises. We thus passed the entire night re-
counting the wonders of the Lord, and consoled each
other in the assurances of our safety.

"Daylight having come, Jacques Ribault, Captain
of the Pearl, boarded us to confer with us respecting

what was to be done by us, and what means we should take for the safety of the rest of our men and the vessels. It was then objected, the small quantity of provisions which we had, our strength broken, our munitions and means of defense taken from us, the uncertainty as to the condition of our Admiral, and not knowing but that he had been shipwrecked on some coast a long distance from us, or driven to a distance by the tempest.

"We thereupon concluded that we could do no better than return to France, and were of the opinion that the company should divide into two parts, the one remaining on board the Pearl, and the other under charge of Captain Maillard.

"On Friday, the twenty-fifth day of the month of September, we departed from this coast, favored by a strong northerly wind, having concluded to return to France, and after the first day our two ships were so far separated that we did not again encounter each other. We proceeded five hundred leagues prosperously, when, one morning about sunrise, we were attacked by a Spanish vessel, which we met as well as we could, and cannonaded them in such sort that we made them subject to our disposal, and battered them so that the blood was seen to overrun the scuppers. We held them then as surrendered and defeated; but there was no means of grappling her, on account of the roughness of the sea, for in grappling her there would be danger of our striking together, which might have sunk us; she also, satisfied with the affair, left us, joyful and thanking God that no one of us was wounded or killed in this skirmish except our cook.

"The rest of our passage was without any rarecounter with enemies; but we were much troubled by contrary winds, which often threatened to cast us on the coast of Spain, which would have been the finishing touch to our misfortunes, and the thing of which we had the greatest horror. We also endured at sea many other things, such as cold and hunger; for be it understood that we, who escaped from the land of Florida, had nothing else for vestment or equipment, by day or by night, except our shirts alone, or some other little rag, which was a small matter of defense from the exposure to the weather; and what was more, the bread which we eat, and we eat it very sparingly, was all spoilt and rotten, as well also the water itself was all noisome, and of which, besides, we could only have for the whole day a single small glass.

"This bad food was the reason, on our landing, that many of us fell into divers maladies, which carried off many of the men of our company; and we arrived at last, after this perilous and lamentable voyage, at

Rochelle; where we were received and treated very humanely and kindly by the inhabitants of the country and those of the city, giving us of their means, to the extent our necessities required; and assisted by their kindness we were each enabled to return to his own part of the country."*

Laudonnière's† narrative speaks more of his own personal escape; and that of Le Moyne‡ refers to this description of De Challeux, as containing a full and accurate account of what took place. Barcia mentions De Challeux very contemptuously as a carpenter, who succeeding badly at his trade took up that of preaching, but does not deny the truth of his narrative. Those who separated from their comrades and threw themselves upon their enemies' mercy, are mentioned by the Spanish writers; but they are silent as to the treatment they received.

---

* Ternaux Compans.   † Hakluyt.   ‡ Brevis Narratio.

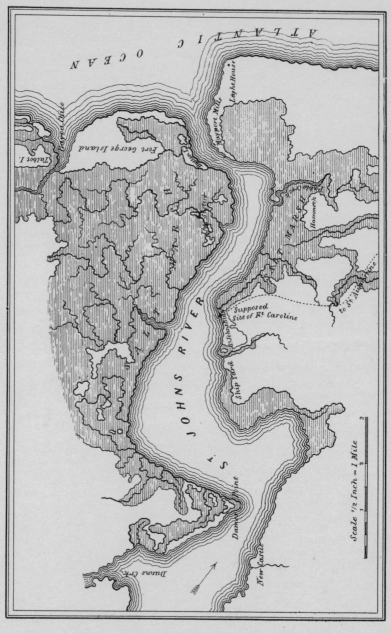

ENTRANCE OF Sᵗ JOHNS RIVER.

Scale ½ Inch = 1 Mile

CHAPTER VI.

SITE OF FORT CAROLINE, AFTERWARDS CALLED SAN MATTEO.

It might naturally be supposed that a spot surrounded with so many thrilling and interesting associations, as the scene of the events we have just related, would have been commemorated either by tradition or by ancient remains attesting its situation. But, in truth, no recognized point now bears the appellation of Fort Caroline, and the antiquary can point at this day to no fosse or parapet, no crumbling bastion, no ancient helm or buckler, no shattered and corroded garniture of war mingled with the bones of the dead, as evidencing its position.

A writer who has himself done more to rescue from oblivion the historical romance of the South than any other,* has well said, "It will be an employment of curious interest, whenever the people of Florida shall happen upon the true site of the settlement and structure of Laudonniere, to trace

---

* W. Gilmore Simms, Esq.

out in detail these several localities, and fix them for the benefit of posterity. The work is scarcely beyond the hammer and chisel of some Old Mortality, who has learned to place his affections and fix his sympathies upon the achievements of the past."

With a consciousness of our unfitness to establish absolutely a memorial so interesting as the site of Fort Caroline must ever be, I shall endeavor to locate its position, upon the basis of reasons entirely satisfactory to myself, and measurably so, I trust, to others.

The account given by Laudonnière himself, the leader of the Huguenots, by whom Fort Caroline was constructed, is as follows:—After speaking of his arrival at the mouth of the river, which had been named the River May by Ribault, who had entered it on the first day of May, 1562, and had therefore given it that name, he says, "Departing from thence, I had not sailed three leagues up the river, still being followed by the Indians, crying still, 'amy,' 'amy,' that is to say, friend, but I discovered an hill of meane height, neare which I went on land, harde by the fieldes that were sowed with mil, at one corner whereof there was an house, built for their lodgings which keep and garde the mil. * * * * * Now was I determined to searche out the qualities of the hill. Therefore I went right

to the toppe thereof; where we found nothing else
but cedars, palms, and bay trees of so sovereign odor
that Balme smelleth not more sweetly. The trees
were environed around about with vines bearing
grapes, in such quantities that the number would
suffice to make the place habitable. Besides the
fertilitie of the soyle for vines, one may see mesquine
wreathed about the trees in great quantities. Touch-
ing the pleasure of the place, the sea may be seen
plain enough from it; and more than six great leagues
off, towards the River Belle, a man may behold the
meadows, divided asunder into isles and islets, enter-
lacing one another. Briefly, the place is so pleasant,
that those which are melancholicke, would be inforced
to change their humour. * * *

" Our fort was built in form of a triangle; the side
towards the west, which was toward the land, was
inclosed with a little trench and raised with turf
made in the form of a battlement, nine feet high ; the
other side, which was towards the river, was inclosed
with a palisade of planks of timber, after the manner
that Gabions are made; on the south line, there was
a kind of bastion, within which I caused an house for
the munition to be made. It was all builded with
fagots and sand, saving about two or three foote
high, with turfes whereof the battlements were made.
In the middest, I caused a great court to be made of

eighteen paces long, and the same in breadth. In
the middest whereof, on the one side, drawing
towards the south, I builded a corps de garde and
an house on the other side towards the north. * *
* * * One of the sides that inclosed my court,
which I made very faire and large, reached unto the
grange of my munitions; and on the other side,
towards the river, was mine own lodgings, round
which were galleries all covered. The principal
doore of my lodging was in the middest of the great
place, and the other was towarde the river. A good
distance from the fort I built an oven."

Jacob Le Moyne, or Jacques Morgues, as he is
sometimes called, accompanied the expedition; and
his *Brevis Narratio* contains two plates, representing
the commencement of the construction of Fort Caroline, and its appearance when completed. The
latter represents a much more finished fortification
than could possibly have been constructed, but may
be taken as a correct outline, I presume, of its general appearance.

Barcia, in his account of its capture, describes
neither its shape nor appearance, but mentions the
parapet nine feet high, and the munition house and
store house.

From the account of Laudonnière and Le Moyne,
it was situated near the river, on the slope or nearly

at the foot of a hill.* Barcia speaks of its being behind a hill, and of descending towards it. The clerical-carpenter, Challeux, speaks of being able, after his escape, to look down from the hill he was on, into the court of the fort itself, and seeing the massacre of the French. As he was flying from the fort towards the sea, and along the river, and as the Spaniards came from a southeast direction, the fort must have been on the westerly side of a hill, near the river.

The distance is spoken of as less than three leagues by Laudonnière. Hawkins and Ribault say, the fort was not visible from the mouth of the river. It is also incidentally spoken of in Barcia as being two leagues from the bar. Le Challeux, in the narrative of his escape, speaks of the distance as being about two leagues. In the account given of the expedition of De Gourgues, it is said to be, in general terms, about one or two leagues above the forts afterwards constructed on each side of the mouth of the river; and it is also mentioned in De Gourgues, that the fort was at the foot of a hill, near the water, and could be overlooked from the hill. The distance from the mouth of the river, and the nature of the ground where the fort was built, are thus made suf-

---

* Laudonnière says, "*joignant la montagne.*"

ficiently definite to enable us to seek a location which shall fulfill both these conditions. It is hardly necessary to remark, that there can be no question but that the fort was located on the south or easterly side of the river, as the Spaniards marched by land from St. Augustine, in a northwesterly direction to Fort Caroline.

The River St. Johns is one of the largest rivers, in point of width, to be found in America, and is more like an arm of the sea than a river; from its mouth for a distance of fifteen miles, it is spread over extensive marshes, and there are few points where the channel touches the banks of the river. At its mouth it is comparatively narrow, but immediately extends itself over wide-spread marshes; and the first headland or shore which is washed by the channel is a place known as St. John's Bluff. Here the river runs closely along the shore, making a bold, deep channel close up to the bank. The land rises abruptly on one side, into a hill of moderate height, covered with a dense growth of pine, cedar, &c. This hill gently slopes to the banks of the river, and runs off to the southwest, where, at the distance of a quarter of a mile, a creek discharges itself into the river, at a place called the Shipyard from time immemorial.

I am not aware that any remains of Fort Caroline,

or any old remains of a fortress, have ever been discovered here; but it must be recollected that this
fort was constructed of sand and pine trees, and that
three hundred years have passed away, with their
storms and tempests, their rains and destructive
influences—a period sufficient to have destroyed a
work of much more durable character than sandy
entrenchments and green pine stakes and timbers.
Moreover, it is highly probable, judging from present
appearances, that the constant abrasion of the banks
still going on has long since worn away the narrow
spot where stood Fort Caroline. It is also to be
remarked, that as there is no other hill, or high land,
or place where a fort could have been built, between
St. John's Bluff and the mouth of the river, so it
is also the fact, that there is no point on the south
side of the river where the channel touches high
land, for a distance by water of eight or ten miles
above St. John's Bluff.

The accompanying diagram and map will illustrate
this point more fully, and starting at St. John's
Bluff, the track of the fugitives, as they crossed the
several creeks, is easily followed, until they reached
the vessels at the mouth of the river.

The evidence in favor of the location of Fort Caroline at St. John's Bluff is, I think, conclusive and
irresistible, and accords in all points with the descrip-

tions given as to distance, topography, and points of view.

It is within the memory of persons now living,* that a considerable orange grove and somewhat extensive buildings, which existed at this place, then called San Vicente, have been washed into the river, leaving at this day no vestiges of their existence. It has been occupied as a Spanish fort within fifty years; yet so rapid has been the work of time and the elements, that no remains of such occupation are now to be seen.

The narratives all speak of·the distance from the mouth of the river as about two leagues; and in speaking of so short a distance the probability of exactness is much greater than when dealing with longer distances.

As to the spot itself, it presents all the natural features mentioned by Laudonnière; and it requires but a small spice of enthusiasm and romance that it be recognized as a "goodlie and pleasante spotte," by those who might like the abundance of the wild grapes and the view of the distant salt meadows, with their "iles and islets, so pleasante that those which are melancholicke would be inforced to change their humour."

---

* Col. T. D. Hart; Mrs. James Smith.

It is but proper, however, to say, that at a plantation known as Newcastle there is a high range of ground, and upon this high ground the appearance of an old earth-work of quadrangular form; but this point is distant some six leagues from the mouth of the river, is flanked by a deep bay or marsh to the southeast, and the work is on the top of the hill and not at its foot, is quadrangular and not triangular, and is a considerable distance from the water. These earth-works, I am satisfied, are Spanish or English remains of a much later period.

CHAPTER VII.

MENENDEZ'S RETURN TO ST. AUGUSTINE—SHIPWRECK OF RI-
BAULT—MASSACRE OF PART OF HIS COMMAND—A. D. 1565.

AFTER an ineffectual attempt to induce those in
the small vessels of the French to surrender, failing
in this, the General concluded to return to St. Augustine, and send two of his vessels to the mouth of
the river to intercept them.

Some of the fugitives from the fort fled to the
Indians; and ten of these were given up to the
Spaniards, to be butchered in cold blood, says the
French account,—to be sent back to France, says the
Spanish chronicle.

The 24th September being the day of St. Matthew,
the name of the fort was changed to that of San
Matheo, by which name it was always subsequently
called by the Spaniards; and the name of St. Matthew
was also given by them to the river, now called St.
Johns, on which it was situated.

The Spaniards proceeded at once to strengthen

the fortress, deepening and enlarging the ditch, and raised and strengthened the ramparts and walls in such manner, says the boastful Mendoza, "that if the half of all France had come to attack it, they could not have disturbed it;" a boast upon which the easy conquest of it by De Gourgues, three years subsequently, affords an amusing commentary. They also constructed, subsequently, two small forts at the mouth of the river, one on each side, which probably were located the one at Batten Island and the other at Mayport.

Leaving three hundred soldiers as a garrison under his son-in-law, De Valdez, Master of the Camp, who was now appointed Governor of the fort, Menendez marched for St. Augustine, beginning now to feel considerable anxiety lest the French fleet, escaping from the tempest, might return and visit upon his own garrison at St. Augustine, the fate of Fort Caroline. He took with him upon his return but fifty soldiers, and, owing to the swollen waters, found great difficulty in retracing his route. When within a league of St. Augustine, he allowed one of the soldiers to go forward to announce his victory and safe return.

The garrison at St. Augustine had been in great anxiety respecting their leader, and from the accounts given by those who had deserted, they had feared the total loss of the expedition. The worthy Chaplain thus describes the return of Menendez:—

"The same day, being Monday, we saw a man coming, crying out loudly. I myself was the first to run to him for the news. He embraced me with transport, crying, 'Victory! Victory! The French fort is ours.' I promised him the present which the bearer of good news deserves, and gave him the best in my power.

"At the hour of vespers our good General arrived, with fifty foot-soldiers very much fatigued. As soon as I learned that he was coming, I ran home and put on a new soutain, the best which I had, and a surplice, and going out with a crucifix in my hand, I went forward to receive him; and he, a gentleman and a good Christian, before entering kneeled and all his followers, and returned thanks to the Lord for the great favours which he had received. My companions and myself marched in front in procession chanting, so that we all returned with the greatest demonstrations of joy."

When about to dispatch the two vessels in his harbor to the St. John's, to cut off the French vessels he had left there, he was informed that two sail had already been seen to pass the bar, supposed to contain the French fugitives.

Eight days after the capture of Fort Caroline, a

fire broke out in the quarters of St. Augustine, which destroyed much treasure and provisions, and the origin of which was doubtful, whether to be ascribed to accident or design. Much disaffection prevailed among the officers and soldiers, and the fire was looked upon with pleasure by some, as having a tendency to hasten their departure from a spot which offered few temptations or rewards, compared with Mexico or Peru.

On the very day of Menendez's return, a Frenchman was discovered by a fishing party on Anastasia Island, who, being taken, said he was one of a party of eighteen, sent in a small vessel, some days before, to reconnoitre the Spanish position; that they had been unable to keep the sea, and had been thrown ashore, about four leagues below, at the mouth of a river; that the Indians attacked and killed three of their number, and they thereupon escaped.

Menendez dispatched a captain and fifty men, to get off the vessel and capture any of the French who might be found. On their arrival at the place, they found that all the French had been killed by the Indians; but they succeeded in getting off the vessel. Menendez, feeling uneasy in reference to their encounter with the Indians, had followed on after the expedition, in company with the worthy Chaplain, to whom his promenade among the briars,

vines, prickly cedars, chaparral, and prickly pears
of Anastasia, seems to have been a true *via dolorosa*.

Upon their arrival, they found a considerable body
of French upon the south side of an inlet, whose
fires indicated their position.

The four vessels of Ribault, which had gone in
pursuit of the Spaniards at St. Augustine, had been
overtaken by the storm, and after keeping to sea
with incredible effort, had been finally driven ashore
upon the shoals of Canaveral,* with but little loss
of life but a total loss of every thing else; they
were thus thrown on shore without shelter from the
elements, famished with hunger, borne down by
disappointment, and utterly dispirited and demoralized. They were consumed, also, by the most painful uncertainty. Marching to the northward along
shore, they discovered a skiff, and resolved to send
a small number of persons in it, to make their way
by sea to Fort Caroline, to bring succor to them from
there. This boat succeeded in reaching the St.
John's, where they were informed, by friendly Indians, of the fate which had befallen the fort; and
subsequently they fell in with a Frenchman who
had escaped, who related to them the whole disaster.

* Canaveral, where Ribault was wrecked, must have been some point
north of Mosquito Inlet, and not the cape now bearing that name, as he
could not have crossed Mosquito Inlet in his march to Matanzas.

Upon this they concluded to seek their own safety among the friendly Indians of St. Helena, rather than to be the useless bearers of the tidings of their misfortunes to their companions in arms.

There are several accounts of the sad fate which befell the followers of Ribault, the massacre of whom has been perpetuated by the memorial name given to its scene, "the bloody river of Matanzas," the ebb and flow of whose recurring tides for three hundred years have failed to wash out the record of blood which has associated this massacre of the Huguenots with the darkest scenes of earth's history. In consequence of the rank and number of the victims, the event produced various and somewhat contradictory accounts; but all stamped with a seal of reprobation and execration the act and the actors, without reference to creed or nationality. Challeux relates instances of cruel barbarity added to the atrocity of the slaughter itself; and others, it appears, had given other versions, all in different degree pointing the finger of historic justice to mark and commemorate the crime against humanity.

The Spanish historian, Barcia, aims to counteract this general condemnation, of which in his own language he says, "These calumnies, repeated in so many quarters, have sullied the fame of the Adelantado, being exaggerated by the heretics, and con-

sented to by the Catholics, so that even the Father
Felix Briot, in his annals, says that he caused them
to be killed contrary to the faith which he had given
them; which is altogether a falsehood, for the Adelantado did not give his word, nor would he when asked
give it, to spare their lives, although they were willing to pay him for doing so; nor in the capture of
Fort Caroline did he do more than has been related;
and such is the account given by Doctor Salis de las
Meras, brother-in-law to Donna Maria de Salis, wife
of the Adelantado, who was present, and who, relating the punishment of the heretics, and the manner
in which it was accomplished, says,—

"'The Adelantado occupied himself in fortifying
his settlement at St. Augustine, as well as he could,
to defend it from the French fleet if they should
attack it. Upon the following day some Indians
came and by signs informed them that four leagues
distant there were a large number of Christians, who
were unable to cross an arm of the sea or strait, which
is a river upon the inner side of an inlet, which they
were obliged to cross in order to come to St. Augustine. The Adelantado sent thither forty soldiers
about dusk, and arrived about midnight near the
inlet, where he commanded a halt until morning, and
leaving his soldiers concealed, he ascended a tree to
see what was the state of matters. He discovered

many persons on the other side of the river, and
their standards; and to prevent their passing over,
he directed his men to exhibit themselves towards
the shore, so that it might be supposed that he had
with him a large force; and when they were discovered, a French soldier swam over, and said that the
persons beyond the river were Frenchmen, that they
had been wrecked in a storm, but had all saved their
lives. The Adelantado asked what French they
were? He answered, that they were two hundred
of the people under command of Jean Ribault,
Viceroy and Captain General of this country for
the king of the French. He asked again, if they
were Catholics or Lutherans? It was replied that
they were all Lutherans, of the new religion; all of
which was previously well known to the Adelantado,
when he encountered their fleet with his vessels; and
the women and children whom he had spared when
he took their fort, had also so informed him; and he
had found in the fort when he took it, six trunks
filled with books, well bound and gilt; all of which
were of the new sect, and from which they did not
say mass, but preached their Lutheran doctrines
every evening; all of which books he directed to be
burnt, not sparing a single one.

" 'The Adelantado then asked him why he had
come over? He said he had been sent over by his

Captain, to see what people they were. The General asked if he wished to return. He said " Yes, but he desired to know what people they were." This man spoke very plainly, for he was a Gascon of San Juan de Suz. " Then tell him," said the Adelantado, "that it is the Viceroy and Captain General of this country for the king, Don Philip; and that his name is Pedro Menendez, and that he is here with some of his soldiery to ascertain what people those were, for he had been informed the day before that they were there, and the hour at which they came."

" ' The French soldier went over with his message, and immediately returned, saying " that if they would pledge faith to his captain and to four other gentlemen, they would like to come and treat with him;" and they desired the loan of a boat, which the General had directed to bring some provisions to the river. The General instructed the messenger to say to his captain, "that he might come over securely under the pledge of his word," and then sent over for them the boat; and they crossed over. The Adelantado received them very well, with only ten of his followers; the others he directed to stay some distance off among some bushes, so that their number might appear to be greater than it was. One of the Frenchmen announced himself as captain of these people; and that in

a great storm they had lost four galleons, and other
vessels of the king of France, within a distance of
twenty leagues of each other ; and that these were
the people from on board of one ship, and that they
desired they would let them have a boat for this
arm of the sea, and for another four leagues hence,
which was at St. Augustine ; that they desired to go
to a fort which they held twenty leagues from there.
It was the same fort which Menendez had taken.
The Adelantado asked them "if they were Catholics
or Lutherans ?" He replied " that they were all of
the New Religion." Then the Adelantado said
to them, " Gentlemen, your fort is taken and its people destroyed, except the women, and children under
fifteen years of age ; and that you may be assured
of this, among the soldiers who are here there are
many things, and also there are here two Frenchmen
whom I have brought with me, who said they were
Catholics. Sit down here and eat, and I will send
the two Frenchmen to you, as also the things which
some of my soldiers have taken from the fort, in
order that you may be satisfied.

" ' The Adelantado having spoken thus, directed
food to be given to them, and sent the two Frenchmen
to them, and many things which the soldiers had
brought from the fort, that they might see them,
and then retired himself, to eat with his own people ;

and an hour afterwards, when he saw that the French had eaten, he went where they were and asked if they were satisfied of the truth of what he had told them. They said they were, and desired that for a consideration, he should give them vessels and ships' stores, that they might return to France. The Adelantado answered, "that he would do so with great pleasure if they were good Catholics, or if he had the ships for them; but he had not the vessels, having sent two to St. Matteo (Ft. Caroline), the one to take the artillery they had captured, and the French women and children, to St. Domingo, and to obtain provisions. The other had to go upon business of his Majesty to other parts.

"'The French captain replied, "that he should grant to all, their lives, and that they should remain with him until they could obtain shipping for France, since they were not at war, and the kings of Spain and of France were brothers and friends." The Adelantado said, "that was true, and Catholics and friends he would favor, believing that he would serve both kings in doing so ; but as to themselves, being of the new sect, he held them for enemies, and he would wage war upon them even to blood and to fire; and that he would pursue them with all cruelty wherever he should encounter them, in whatever sea or land where he should be viceroy or captain general for his king; and that he would go and plant the holy faith in this land, that the Indians might be enlightened and be brought to the knowledge of the Holy Catholic Faith of Jesus Christ our Saviour, as taught and announced by the Roman Church. That if they wished to surrender their standards and their arms, and throw themselves upon his mercy, they might do so, for *he would do with them what God should of his grace direct;* or, they could do as they might deem proper; that other treaty or friendship they should not have from him." The French captain replied, that he could not then conclude any other matter with the Adelantado. He went over in the boat, saying, that he went to relate what had passed, and to agree upon what should be done, and within two hours he would return with an answer. The Adelantado said, " They could do as seemed best to them, and he would wait for them." Two hours passed, when the same French captain returned, with those who had accompanied him previously, and said to the General, " that there were many people of family, and nobles among them, and that they would give fifty thousand ducats, of ransom, if he would spare all their lives." He answered, " that although he was a poor soldier, he could not be governed by selfish interests, and if he were to be merciful and lenient, he desired to be so without the suspicion of other motives." The French captain returned to urge the matter. " Do not deceive yourselves," said the Adelantado, " for if Heaven were to join to earth, I would do no otherwise than I have said." The French officer then going towards where his people stood, said, that in accordance with that understanding he would return shortly with an answer; and within half an hour he returned and placed in the boat, the standards, seventy arquebuses, twenty pistols, a quantity of swords and shields, and some helmets and breast-plates; and the captain came to where the General stood, and said that all the French force there submitted themselves to his clemency, and surrendered to him their standards and their arms. The Adelantado then directed twenty soldiers to go in the boat and bring the French, ten by ten. The river was narrow and easy to pass, and he directed Diego Flores de Valdes, Admiral of the Fleet, to receive the standards and the arms, and to go in the boat and see that the soldiers did not maltreat them. The Adelantado then withdrew from the shore, about two bow shots, behind a hillock of sand, within a copse of bushes, where the persons who came in the boat which brought over the French, could not see; and then said to the French captain and the other eight Frenchmen who were there with him, " Gentlemen, I have but few men with me, and

they are not very effective, and you are numerous;
and, going unrestrained, it would be an easy thing
to take satisfaction upon our men for those whom
we destroyed when we took the fort; and thus it is
necessary that you should march with hands tied
behind, a distance of four leagues from here where
I have my camp." The French replied "that they
would do so;" and they had their hands tied
strongly behind their backs with the match ropes of
the soldiers; and the ten who came in the boat did
not see those who had their hands tied, until they
came up to the same place, for it was so arranged,
in order that the French who had not passed the
river, should not understand what was being done,
and might not be offended, and thus were tied two
hundred and eight Frenchmen. Of whom the Adelantado asked that if any among them were Catholics, they should declare it. Eight said that they
were Catholics, and were separated from the others
and placed in a boat, that they might go by the
river to St. Augustine; and all the rest replied "that
they were of the new religion, and held themselves
to be very good Christians; that this was their
faith and no other. The Adelantado then gave the
order to march with them, having first given them
meat and drink, as each ten arrived, before being
tied, which was done before the succeeding ten

6

arrived; and he directed one of his captains who marched with the vanguard, that at a certain distance from there, he would observe a mark made by a lance, which he carried in his hand, which would be in a sandy place that they would be obliged to pass in going on their way towards the fort of St. Augustine, and that there the prisoners should all be destroyed; and he gave the one in command of the rear-guard the same orders; and it was done accordingly; when, leaving there all of the dead, they returned the same night before dawn, to the fort at St. Augustine, although it was already sundown when the men were killed.'" *

Such is the second part of this sad and bloody tragedy; which took place at the Matanzas Inlet, about eighteen miles south of the city of St. Augustine, and at the southerly end of Anastasia Island. The account we have given, it must be borne in mind, is that of De Solis, the brother-in-law and apologist of Menendez; but even under his extenuating hand the conduct of Menendez was that of one deaf to the voice of humanity, and exulting in cold-blooded treachery, dealing in vague generalities intended to deceive, while affording a shallow apology for the actor. A massacre in cold blood of poor ship-

---

* Barcia, p. 87.

wrecked, famished men, prisoners yielding themselves to an expected clemency, tied up like sheep, and butchered by poignard blows from behind, shocked alike the moral sense of all to whom the tale came, without regard to faith or flag.

CHAPTER VIII.

FATE OF RIBAULT AND HIS FOLLOWERS—BLOODY MASSACRE
AT MATANZAS—1565.

THE first detachment of the French whom Menendez met and so utterly destroyed, constituted the complement of a single vessel, which had been thrown ashore at a more northerly point than the others. All these vessels were wrecked between Musquito Inlet and Matanzas.

Of the fate of the main detachment, under Ribault in person, we have the following account, as related by the same apologist, the chaplain De Solis:

"On the next day following the return of the Adelantado at St. Augustine, the same Indians who came before returned, and said that 'a great many more Christians were at the same part of the river as the others had been.' The Adelantado concluded that it must be Jean Ribault, the General of the Lutherans at sea and on land, whom they called the Viceroy of this country for the king of France. He immediately went, with one hundred and fifty men in good order, and reached the place where he had lodged the first time, at about midnight; and at dawn he pushed forward to the river, with his men drawn out, and when it was daylight, he saw, two bow-shots from the other bank of the river, many persons, and a raft made to cross over the people, at the place where the Adelantado stood. But immediately, when the French saw the Adelantado and his people, they took arms, and displayed a royal standard and two standards of companies, sounding fifes and drums, in very good order, and showing a front of battle to the Adelantado; who, having ordered his men to sit down and take their breakfast, so that they made no demonstration of any change, he himself walked up and down the shore, with his admiral and two other captains, paying no attention to the movement and demonstration of battle of the French; so that they, observing this, halted and the fifes and drums ceased, while with a bugle note they unfurled the white flag of peace, which was returned by the Adelantado. A Frenchman placed himself upon the raft, and cried with a loud voice that he wished to cross over, but that owing to the force of the current he could not bring the raft over, and desired an Indian canoe which was there to be sent over. The Adelantado said he could swim over for it, under pledge of his word.

A French sailor immediately came over, but the General would not permit him to speak with him, but directed him to take the canoe, and go and tell his captain, that inasmuch as he had called for a conference, if he desired any thing he should send over some one to communicate with him. The same sailor immediately came with a gentleman, who said he was the sergeant major of Jean Ribault, Viceroy and Captain General of this land for the king of France, and that he had sent him to say, that they had been wrecked with their fleet in a great storm, and that he had with him three hundred and fifty French; that they wished to go to a fort which they held, twenty leagues from there; that they wished the favor of boats, to pass this river, and the other, four leagues further on, and that he desired to know if they were Spaniards, and under what leader they served.

"The Adelantado answered him, that they were Spaniards, and that the Captain under whom they served was the person now addressing him, and was called Pedro Menendez. That he should tell his General that the fort which he held twenty leagues from there had been taken by him, and he had destroyed all the French, and the rest who had come with the fleet, because they were badly governed; and then, passing thence to where the dead bodies of the

Frenchmen whom he had killed still lay unburied, pointed them out to him and said, therefore he could not permit them to pass the river to their fort.

"The sergeant, with an unmoved countenance, and without any appearance of uneasiness on account of what the Adelantado had said, replied, that if he would have the goodness to send a gentleman of his party, to say to the French general, that they might negotiate with safety, the people were much exhausted, and the general would come over in a boat which was there. The Adelantado replied, 'Farewell, comrade, and bear the answer which they shall give you; and if your general desires to come and treat with me, I give my word that he shall come and return securely, with four or six of his people whom he may select for his advisors, that he may do whatever he may conclude to be best.'

"The French gentleman then departed with this message. Within half an hour he returned to accept the assurance the Adelantado had given, and to obtain the boat; which the Adelantado was unwilling to let him have, but said he could use the canoe, which was safe, and the strait was narrow; and he again went back with this message.

"Immediately Jean Ribault came over, whom the Adelantado received very well, with other eight gentlemen, who had come with him. They were all gentlemen of rank and position. He gave them a collation, and would have given them food if they had desired. Jean Ribault with much humility, thanked him for his kind reception, and said that to raise their spirits, much depressed by the sad news of the death of their comrades, they would partake only of the wine and condiments, and did not wish any thing else to eat. Then after eating, Jean Ribault said, 'that he saw that those his companions were dead, and that he could not be mistaken if he desired to be.' Then the Adelantado directed the soldiers to bring each one whatever he had taken from the fort; and he saw so many things, that he knew for certain that it was taken; although he knew this before, yet he could not wholly believe it, because among his men there was a Frenchman by name of Barbero, of those whom the Adelantado had ordered to be destroyed with the rest, and who was left for dead with the others, having with the first thrust he received fallen down and made as though he were dead, and when they left there he had passed over by swimming, to Ribault; and this Barbero held it for certain that the Adelantado had deceived them in saying that the fort was taken, it not being so; and thus until now he had supposed. The Adelantado said that in order with more certainty to believe this and satisfy himself, he might converse

apart with the two Frenchmen who were present, to
satisfy him better ; which he did.

"Immediately Jean Ribault came towards the
Adelantado and said, 'it was certain that all which
he had told him was true ; but that what had happened
to him, might have happened to the Adelantado ;
and since their kings were brothers, and such great
friends, the Adelantado should act towards him as a
friend, and give him ships and provisions, that he
might return to France.'

"The Adelantado replied in the same manner that
he had done to the other Frenchmen, as to what he
would do ; and that taking it or leaving it, Jean
Ribault could obtain nothing further from the Adelantado. Jean Ribault then said that he would go
and give an account of matters to his people, for he
had among them many of noble blood ; and would
return or send an answer as to what he would do.

"Three hours afterwards, Jean Ribault returned
in the canoe, and said, 'that there were different
opinions among his people; that while some were
willing to yield themselves to his clemency, others
were not.' The Adelantado replied 'that it mat-
tered but little to him whether they all came, or a
part, or none at all ; that they should do as it pleased
them, and he would act with the same liberty.'
Jean Ribault said to him, 'that the half of the peo-

ple who were willing to yield themselves to his clemency, would pay him a ransom of more than 100,000 ducats; and the other half were able to pay more, for there was among them persons of wealth and large incomes, who had desired to establish estates in this country.' The Adelantado answered him, 'It would grieve me much to lose so great and rich a ransom, under the necessity I am under for such aid, to carry forward the conquest and settlement of this land, in the name of my king, as is my duty, and to plant here the Holy Evangel.' Jean Ribault considered from this, that with the amount which they could all give, he might be induced to spare his own life and that of all the others who were with him, and that they might be able to pay more than 200,000 ducats; and he said to the Adelantado, 'that he would return with his answer to his people; that as it was late, he would take it as a favor if he would be willing to wait until the following day, when he would bring their reply as to what they would conclude to do.' The Adelantado said, 'Yes, that he would wait.' Jean Ribault then went back to his people, it being already sunset. In the morning, he returned with the canoe, and surrendered to the Adelantado two royal standards—the one that of the king of France, the other that of the Admiral (Coligny),—and the standards of the company, and a sword, dagger, and helmet, gilded very beautifully; and also a shield, a pistol, and a commission given him under the high admiral of France, to assure to him his title and possessions.

"He then said to him, 'that but one hundred and fifty of the three hundred and fifty whom he had with him were willing to yield to his clemency, and that the others had withdrawn during the night; and that they might take the boat and bring those who were willing to come over, and their arms.' The Adelantado immediately directed the captain, Diego Flores Valdes, Admiral of the fleet, that he should bring them over as he had done the others, ten by ten; and the Adelantado, taking Jean Ribault behind the sand hills, among the bushes where the others had their hands tied behind them, he said to these and all the others as he had done before, that they had four leagues to go after night, and that he could not permit them to go unbound; and after they were all tied, he asked if they were Catholics or Lutherans, or if any of them desired to make confession.

"Jean Ribault replied, 'that all who were there were of the new religion,' and he then began to repeat the psalm, '*Domine! Memento Mei;*' and having finished, he said, 'that from dust they came and to dust they must return, and that in twenty

years, more or less, he must render his final account;
that the Adelantado might do with them as he
chose.' The Adelantado then ordered all to be
killed, in the same order and at the same mark, as
had been done to the others. He spared only the
fifers, drummers, and trumpeters, and four others
who said that they were Catholics, in all, sixteen
persons." " *Todos los demas fueron degallados,*"—
" all the rest were slaughtered," is the sententious
summary by which Padre de Solis announced the
close of the sad career of the gray-haired veteran,
the brave soldier, the Admiral Jean Ribault, and his
companions.*

At some point on the thickly-wooded shores of
the Island of Anastasio, or beneath the shifting
mounds of sand which mark its shores, may still lie
the bones of some of the three hundred and fifty
who, spared from destruction by the tempest, and
escaping the perils of the sea and of the savage, fell
victims to the vindictive rancor and blind rage of
one than whom history recalls none more cruel, or
less humane. But while their bones, scattered on
earth and sea, unhonored and unburied, were lost to
human sight, the tale of their destruction and sad
fate, scattered in like manner over the whole world,

---

* Barcia, p. 89.

has raised to their memory through sympathy with
their fate, a memorial which will endure as long as
the pages of history.

The Adelantado returned that night to St. Augustine, where, says his apologist, some persons censured
him for his cruelty. Others commended what he had
done, as the act of a good general, and said that even
if they had been Catholics, he could not have done
more justly than he had done for them; for with the
few provisions that the Adelantado had, either the
one or the other people would have had to perish
with hunger, and the French would have destroyed
our people: they were the most numerous.*

We have still to trace the fate of the body of two
hundred, who retired from Ribault after his fatal
determination to surrender to the tender mercies of
Menendez. As we are already aware, it comprised
the elite of his force, men of standing and rank, and
whose spirits had retained the energy to combat
against the natural discouragements of their position;
and they adopted the nobler resolve of selling their
lives, at least with their swords in their hands.

De Solis proceeds to give the following further
account of them:—

"Twenty days subsequently to the destruction of

---

* Barcia, p. 89.

these, some Indians came to the Adelantado, and
informed him by signs, that eight days' journey from
here to the southward, near the Bahama Channel, at
Canaveral, a large number of people, brethren of
those whom the General had caused to be killed,
were building a fort and a vessel. The Adelantado
at once came to the conclusion, that the French had
retired to the place where their vessels were wrecked,
and where their artillery and munitions, and provisions were, in order to build a vessel and return to
France to procure succor. The General thereupon
dispatched from St. Augustine to St. Matteo, ten of
his soldiers, conveying intelligence of what had taken
place, and directing that they should send to him one
hundred and fifty of the soldiers there, with the
thirty-five others who remained when he returned
to St. Augustine, after taking the fort. The master
of the camp immediately dispatched them, under
command of Captains Juan Velez de Medrano and
Andrez Lopez Patrio; and they arrived at St. Augustine on October 23d. On the 25th, after having
heard mass, the Adelantado departed for the coast,
with three hundred men, and three small vessels to
go by sea with the arms and provisions; and the
vessels were to go along and progress equally with
the troops; and each night when the troops halted,

the vessels also anchored by them, for it was a clear and sandy coast.

"The Adelantado carried in the three vessels, provisions for forty days for three hundred men, and one days' ration was to last for two days; and he promised to do everything for the general good of all, although they might have to undergo many dangers and privations; that he had great hope that he would have the goodness and mercy of God to aid him in carrying through safely this so holy and pious an undertaking. He then took leave of them, leaving most of them in tears, for he was much loved, feared, and respected by all.*

"The Adelantado, after a wearisome journey, marching on foot himself the whole distance, arrived in the neighborhood of the French camp on All Saints Day, at daylight, guided by the Indians by land, and the three vessels under the command of Captain Diego de Maya. As soon as the French descried the Spaniards, they fled to their fort, without any remaining. The Adelantado sent them a trumpeter, offering them their lives, that they should return and should receive the same treatment as the Spaniards. One hundred and fifty came to the Adelantado; and their leader, with twenty others,

---

* Barcia, p. 89.

sent to say that they would sooner be devoured by
the Indians, than surrender themselves to the Spaniards. The Adelantado received those who surrendered, very well, and having set fire to the fort,
which was-of wood, burned the vessel which they
were building, and buried the artillery, for the
vessels could not carry them."

De Solis here closes his account of the matter; but
from other accounts we learn that the Adelantado
kept his faith on this occasion with them, and that
some entered his service, some were converted to his
faith, and others returned to France; and thus
ended the Huguenot attempt to colonize the shores
of Florida.

There are several other accounts of the fate of
Ribault and his followers, drawn from the narratives
of survivors of the expedition, which, without vary-
ing the general order of events, fill in sundry details of
the massacres. The main point of difference is, as to
the pledges or assurances given by Menendez. The
French accounts say that he pledged his faith to
them, that their lives should be spared.* It will be
seen that the Spanish account denies that he did so,
but makes him use language subject to misconstruc-

---

* Such was the understanding of those who then wrote in reference
to the transaction, as Barcia admits.

tion, and calculated to deceive them into the hope
and expectation of safety. I do not see that in a
Christian or even moral view there is much difference
between an open breach of faith, and the breach of
an implied faith, particularly when it was only by
this deception that the surrender could have been
accomplished. Nor could Menendez have had a very
delicate sense of the value of the word of a soldier,
a Christian, and a gentleman, when, as his apologist
admits, he did directly use the language of falsehood,
to induce them to submit to the degradation of having their hands tied.

Nor, considered in its broader aspects, is it a matter
of any consequence, whether he gave his word or no;
nor does it lessen the enormity of his conduct, had
they submitted themselves in the most unreserved
manner to his discretion. France and Spain were
at peace; no act of hostility had been committed by
the French toward the Spaniards; and Ribault asked
only to be allowed to pass on. In violation alike
of the laws of war and the law of humanity, he first
induced them to surrender, to abide what God,
whose holy name he invoked, should put into his
heart to do, and then cajoling them into allowing
their hands to be tied, he ordered them to be killed,
in their bonds as they stood, defenseless, helpless,
wrecked, and famished men. It would have been a

7

base blot upon human nature, had he thus served
the most savage tribe of nations, standing on that
far shore, brought into the common sympathy of
want and suffering. The act seems one of monstrous
atrocity, when committed against the people of a
sister nation.

CHAPTER IX.

FORTIFYING OF ST. AUGUSTINE—DISAFFECTIONS AND MUTI-
NIES—APPROVAL OF MENENDEZ' ACTS BY KING OF SPAIN.
1565-1568.

DURING the time of the several expeditions of the
Adelantado against the French Huguenots, the fortification and strengtheni ng of the defenses of the
settlement at St. Augustine had not been neglected.
The fort, or Indian council-house, which had been
first fortified, seems to have been consumed in the
conflagration spoken of; and thereupon a plan of a
regular fortification or fort was marked out by
Menendez; and, as there existed some danger of the
return of the French, the Spaniards labored unceas-
ingly with their whole force, to put it in a respectable
state of defense. From an engraving contained in
De Bry, illustrating the attack of Sir Francis Drake,
twenty years afterwards, this fort appears to have
been an octagonal structure of logs, and located near
the site of the present fort, while the settlement itself
was probably made in the first instance, at the lower

end of the peninsula, near the building now called the powder-house.

He also established a government for the place, with civil and military officials, a hall of justice, et cetera.

All of these matters were arranged by Menendez before his expedition against the French at Canaveral, of whom one hundred and fifty returned with him, and were received upon an equal footing with his own men, the more distinguished being received at his own table upon the most friendly terms ; a clemency which, with a knowledge of his character, can only be ascribed to motives of policy. The position of the French at Canaveral was probably inaccessible, as they had their arms, besides artillery brought from the vessels ; and the duplicity which had characterized his success with their comrades, was out of the question here ; the French could therefore exact their own terms, and unshackled could forcibly resist any attempt at treachery.

The addition of this number to his force lessened the already diminished supply of provisions which Menendez had brought with him ; and want soon began to threaten his camp. He sent as many of his soldiers as he could into camp at San Matteo, and endeavored to draw supplies from the Indians ; but unfortunately for him, the country between the St.

Johns and St. Augustine was under the rule of the Indian Chief, Satouriara, the friend (and ally of the French), whose hostility the Spaniards were never able to overcome. Satouriara and his followers withdrew from all peaceable intercourse with the Spaniards, and hung about their path to destroy, harrass, and cut them off upon every possible occasion.

The winter succeeding the settlement of the Spaniards at St. Augustine, was most distressing and discouraging to them. The lack of provisions in their camp drove them to seek, in the surrounding country, subsistence from the roots and esculent plants it might afford, or to obtain in the neighboring creeks, fish and oysters; but no sooner did a Spaniard venture out alone beyond the gates of the fort, than he was grasped, by some unseen foe, from the low underbrush and put to death, or a shower of arrows from some tree-top was his first intimation of danger; if he discharged his arquebuse towards his invisible assailants, others would spring upon him before he could reload his piece; or, if he attempted to find fish and oysters in some quiet creek, the noiseless canoe of an Indian would dart in upon him, and the heavy war-club of the savage descending upon his unprotected head, end his existence. Against such a foe, no defense could avail; and it is related that more than one hundred and twenty of the Spaniards were thus killed, including Captain Martin de Ochoa, Captain Diego de Hevia, Fernando de Gamboa, and Juan Menendez, a nephew of the Adelantado, and many others of the bravest and most distinguished of the garrison.

In this crisis of affairs, the Governor concluded to go to Cuba himself, to obtain relief for his colony. He in the meantime established a fort at St. Lucia, near Canaveral. A considerable jealousy seems to have existed on the part of the governor of Cuba; and he received Menendez with great coolness, and in reply to his appeals for aid, only offered an empty vessel. In this emergency, Menendez contemplated, as his only means of obtaining what he wished, to go upon a filibustering expedition against some Portuguese and English vessels which were in those waters. While making preparations to do this, four vessels of the fleet with which he had left Spain, and which had been supposed lost, arrived; and after dispatching a vessel to Campeachy for provisions, he commenced his return voyage to his colony, delaying however for a time in South Florida, to seek intelligence among the Indians of his lost son.

In the mean time his garrisons at St. Augustine and San Matteo had mutinied, and were in open revolt; provisions had become so scarce that twenty-five reals had been given for a pound of biscuit, and but for the fish they would have starved. They plundered the public stores, imprisoned their officers, and seized upon a vessel laden with provisions which had been sent to the garrison. The Master of the Camp succeeded in escaping from confinement and releasing his fellow prisoners, by a bold movement cut off the intercourse between the mutineers on board the vessel and those on shore, and hung the Sergeant Major, who was at the head of the movement. The Commandant then attempted to attack those in the vessel, and was nearly lost with his companions, by being wrecked on the bar. The vessel made sail to the West India Islands. The garrison at San Matteo took a vessel there and came around to St. Augustine, but arrived after their accomplices had left.

Disease had already begun to make its ravages, and added to the general wish to leave the country; which all would then have done had they had the vessels in which to embark. They used for their recovery from sickness, the roots of a native shrub, which produced marvelous cures.

At this period Menendez returned to the famished garrison, but was forced to permit Juan Vicente, with one hundred of the disaffected, to go to St. Domingo by a vessel which he dispatched there for supplies; and it is said that the governors of the islands where they went, harbored them, and that of some five hundred who on different occasions deserted from the Adelantado, and all of whom had been brought out at his cost, but two or three were ever returned to him; while the deserters putting their own construction upon their acts, sent home to the king of Spain criminations of the Adelantado, and represented the conquest of Florida as a hopeless and worthless acquisition; that it was barren and swampy, and produced nothing.

After this defection, Menendez proceeded along the coast to San Matteo, and thence to Guale, Amelia, and adjoining islands, Orista and St. Helena; made peaceful proposals to the Indian tribes, lectured them upon theology, and planted a cross at their council-houses. The cacique of Guale asked Menendez how it was "that he had waged war upon the other white men, who had come from the same country as himself?" He replied, "that the other white people were bad Christians, and believers in lies; and that those whom he had killed, deserved the most cruel death, because they had fled their own country, and came to mislead and deceive the caciques and other Indians, as they had already before misled and deceived many other good Christians, in order that the devil may take possession of them." While at St. Helena he succeeded in obtaining permission of the Indians to erect a fort there, and he left a detachment. On his return he also erected fort San Felipe, at Orista; and after setting up a cross at Guale, the cacique demanded of him, that as now they had become good Christians, he should cause rain to come upon their fields; for a drought had continued eight months. The same night a severe rain-storm happened, which confirmed the faith of the Indians, and gained the Adelantado great credit with them. While here, he learned that there was a fugitive Lutheran among the Indians, and he took some pains to cause to be given to the fugitive, hopes of good treatment if he would come in to the Spanish post at St. Helena, while he gave private directions that he should be killed, directing his lieutenant to make very strange of his disappearance; an incident very illustrative of the vindictiveness and duplicity of Menendez.*

He returned to St. Augustine, and was received with great joy, and devoted himself to the completion of the fort, which was to frighten the savages, and enforce respect from strangers. It was built, it is said, where it now stands, *donde este ahora*, (1722.) The colony left at St. Helena mutinied almost

---

* Ensay. Cron. 110.

immediately, and seizing a vessel sent with supplies, sailed for Cuba, and were wrecked on the Florida Keys, where they met at an Indian town, the mutineers who had deserted from the fort at St. Matteo: these had been also wrecked there.

The garrison again becoming much straitened for provisions, the Adelantado, in June, was obliged to go to Cuba for succor. He was received with indifference, and his wishes unheeded. He applied to the governor of Mexico, and others who happened to be there, and who had the power of assisting him; from all he received no encouragement, but the advice to abandon his enterprise. He at last pawned his jewels, the badge of his order, and his valuables, thus obtaining five hundred ducats; with which he purchased provisions, and set sail on his return, with only sixty-five men.

But just at this period, succor came to the famished troops; a fleet of seventeen vessels arrived with fifteen hundred men from Spain, under Juan de Avila, as admiral. By this means all the posts were succored and reinforced, and the enterprise saved from destruction; for the small supplies brought by Menendez would have been soon exhausted, and further efforts being out of his power, they would have been forced to withdraw from the country.

The admiral of the fleet also had entrusted to him for the Adelantado, a letter from the king, written on the 12th of May, 1566, which, among other matters, contained the following royal commendation of the acts of Menendez. "Of the great success which has attended your enterprise, we have the most entire satisfaction, and we bear in memory . the loyalty, the love, and the diligence, with which you have borne us service, as well as the dangers and perils in which you have been placed; and as to the *retribution* you have visited upon the Lutheran pirates who sought to occupy that country, and to fortify themselves there, in order to disseminate in it their wicked creed, and to prosecute there their wrongs and robberies, which they have done and were doing against God's service and my own, we believe that you did it with every justification and propriety, and we consider ourself to have been well served in so doing."*

To this commendation of Philip II., it is unnecessary to add any comment, save that no other action could have been expected of him. And of Charles the Ninth, of France, the Spanish historian says that he treated the memorial of the widows and orphans of the slain with contempt, "considering their pun-

---

* Ensayo: Cron. 115.

ishment to have been just, in that they were equally enemies of Spain, of France, of the Church, and of the peace of the world."

During the absence of Menendez to inspect his posts, disaffection again broke out; and finding his force too numerous, he with sixteen vessels went upon a freebooting expedition to attack pirates. He failed to meet with any; but having learned that a large French fleet was on its way, he visited and fortified the forts on the islands of Cuba, Hispaniola, and Puerto Rico, and again returned to Florida; the expected French fleet never having arrived. About this time, a small vessel brought from Spain three learned and exemplary priests; one of whom, Padre Martinez, landed upon the coast with some of the crew, and being unable to regain the vessel, coasted along to St. George Island, where he was attacked and murdered by the Indians, with a number of his companions.

The following year was principally occupied by Menendez, in strengthening his fortifications at his three forts, in visiting the Indian chiefs at their towns, and exploring the country. One of his expeditions went as far north as the thirty-seventh degree of latitude by sea, and another went to the foot of the Apalachian Mountains, about one hundred and fifty leagues, and established a fort. The former was about the mouth of the Chesapeake, called the Santa Maria; * and the land expedition, probably to the up-country of Georgia, in the neighborhood of Rome.

All attempts at pacifying their warlike neighbor, were as fruitless as their attempts to subjugate him ; whether in artifice and duplicity, in open warfare, or secret ambush, he was more than equal to the Adelantado, and was a worthy ancestor of the modern Seminole,—never present when looked for, and never absent when an opportunity of striking a blow occurred.

The Adelantado having had built an extremely slight vessel of less than twenty tons, called a frigate, concluded to visit Spain, and ran in seventeen days to the Azores, sailing seventy leagues per day, an exploit not often equaled in modern times. He was received with great joy in Spain, and the king treated him with much consideration. The Adelantado felt great anxiety to return to his colony, and deprecated the delays of the court, fearing the result of the indignation at his cruelty to the Huguenots, which, says his chronicler, increased day by day.†

---

* Pensacola Bay was also so called.

† Ensayo : Cron. 133.

CHAPTER X.

THE NOTABLE REVENGE OF DOMINIC DE GOURGUES—RETURN
OF MENENDEZ—INDIAN MISSION—1568.

WHILE Menendez thus remained at the Spanish
court urging the completion of his business, seeking
compensation for the great expenditures which he
had made in the king's service, and vindicating himself from the accusations which had been preferred
against him,—the revenge, the distant murmurs of
which had already reached his ears, fell upon the
Spaniards on the St. Johns.

Dominic de Gourgues, one of those soldiers of fortune, who then abounded throughout Europe, took
upon himself the expression of the indignation with
which the French nation viewed the slaughter of
of their countrymen. From motives of policy, or
from feelings, still less creditable, the French court
ignored the event; but it rankled nevertheless in the
national heart, and many a secret vow of revenge
was breathed, the low whispers of which reached
even the confines of the Spanish court. Conscience,

and the knowledge that the sentiment of the age was against him, made Menendez from the moment of his success exceedingly anxious lest well-merited retribution should fall upon his own colony. He guarded against it in every way in his power: he strengthened all his posts; he erected for the protection of San Matteo, formerly Fort Caroline, two small forts on either side of the entrance of the river, at the points now known as Batten Island and Mayport Mills. He placed large garrisons at each post, and had made such arrangements against surprise or open attack upon his forts, that Father Mendoza boasted that "half of all France could not take them."

De Gourgues, with three vessels and about two hundred and fifty chosen men animated with like feelings with himself, appeared in April, 1568, off the mouth of the St. Johns. The Spanish fort received his vessels with a salute, supposing them to be under the flag of Spain. De Gourgues returned the salute, thus confirming their error. He then entered the St. Marys, called the Somme, and was met by a large concourse of Indians, friendly to the French and bitterly hostile to the Spaniards, at the head of whom was the stern and uncompromising Saturioura. Their plans were quickly formed, and immediately carried into execution. Their place of rendezvous was the Fort George Inlet, called by them the Sarabay; and they traversed that island at low tide, fell suddenly upon the fort at Batten Island on the north side of the river, completely surprising it. The force occupying the Spanish forts amounted to four hundred men, one hundred and twenty of whom occupied the two forts at the mouth of the river, and the remainder Fort Caroline. The French with their Indian allies approached the fort on the north side of the river at day-break. Having waded the intervening marsh and creek to the great damage of their feet and legs by reason of the oyster banks, they arrived within two hundred yards of the post when they were discovered by the sentinel upon the platform of the fort; who immediately cried, "to arms," and discharged twice at the French a culverin which had been taken at Fort Caroline. Before he could load it a third time the brave Olatocara leaped upon him, and killed him with a pike. Gourgues then charging in, the garrison by this time alarmed rushed out, armed hastily and seeking escape; another part of Gourgues' force coming up, inclosed the Spaniards between them, and all but fifteen of the garrison perished on the spot; the others were taken prisoners, only to be reserved for the summary vengeance which the French leader meditated.

The Spanish garrison in the other fort kept up

in the mean time a brisk cannonade, which incommoded the assailants, who however soon managed to point the pieces of the fort they had taken; and under the cover of this fire the French crossed to the other fort, their Indian allies in great numbers swimming with them. The garrison of sixty men, panic-struck, made no attempt at resistance, but fled, endeavoring to reach the main fort; being intercepted by the Indians in one direction, and by the French in another, but few made good their escape. These, arriving at Fort Caroline, carried an exaggerated account of the number of their assailants.

De Gourgues at once pushed forward to attack Fort Caroline, while its defenders were terrified at the suddenness of his attack, and the supposed strength of his force. Upon his arrival near the fort, the Spanish commander sent out a detachment of sixty men, to make a reconnoisance. De Gourgues skillfully interposed a body of his own men with a large number of the Indians between the reconnoitering party and the fort, and then with his main force charged upon them in front; when the Spaniards turning to seek the shelter of the fort, were met by the force in their rear, and were all either killed or taken prisoners. Seeing this misfortune, the Spanish commander despaired of being able to hold the fortress, and determined to make a timely retreat to St.

8

Augustine. In attempting this, most of his followers fell into the hands of the Indians, and were slain upon the spot; the commandant with a few others alone escaped.

De Gourgues, now completely successful in making retaliation for the fate of his countrymen on the same spot where they had suffered, on the same tree which had borne the bodies of the Huguenots caused his prisoners to be suspended; and as Menendez had on the former occasion erected a tablet that they had been punished "not as Frenchmen but as Lutherans," so De Gourgues in like manner erected an inscription that he had done this to them "*not as to Spaniards, nor as to outcasts, but as to traitors, thieves, and murderers.*" *

After inducing the Indians to destroy the forts, and to raze them to the ground, he set sail for France, arriving safely without further adventure.

His conduct was at the time disavowed and censured by the French court; and the Spanish ambassador had the assurance, in the name of that master who had publicly declared his approval of the conduct of Menendez, to demand the surrender of De Gourgues to his vengeance. The brave captain, however the crown might seem to disapprove, was

---

* Ternaux Compans, p. 357.

secretly sustained and protected by many distinguished persons official and private, and by the mass of the people; to whom his boldness, spirit, and signal success were grateful. Some years afterwards, he was restored to the favor of his sovereign, and appointed admiral of the fleet.

That De Gourgues deserves censure, cannot be denied; but there will always exist an admiration for his courage and intrepid valor, with a sympathy for the bitter provocations under which he acted, both personal and national; a sympathy not shared with Menendez, who visited his wrath upon the religious opinions of men, while De Gourgues was the unauthorized avenger of undoubted crime and inhumanity. Both acted in violation of the pure spirit of that Christianity which they alike professed to revere, under the same form.

While these scenes were enacting on the St. Johns, Menendez was upon his way to his colonies, where he first heard of the descent of De Gourgues, then on his way back to France. The Adelantado upon his arrival found his troops hungry and naked, and their relations with the Indians worse than ever. Having made such arrangements as were in his power, he returned to Havana, to further his plans for introducing Christianity among the Indians; to which, to his credit be it said, he devoted the greater share of his time and attention. Father Rogel applied himself to learning their language, with great success; and an institution was established in Havana especially for their instruction. In the Ensayo Cronologica, there is set forth in full, a rescript addressed by Pope Pius V., to Menendez, conveying to him the acknowledgments of his Holiness, for the zeal and loyalty he had exhibited, and his labors in carrying the faith to the Indians, and urging him strongly to see to it, that his Indian converts should. not be scandalized by the vicious lives of their white brethren who claimed to be Christians.

A small party of Spaniards, as has already been mentioned, accompanied by a priest, De Quiros, had been left upon the Chesapeake, and under the auspices of a young converted chief, who had been some time with the Spaniards in Havana and Florida, anticipated a more easy access to the Indian tribes in that region. Another priest, with ten associates, went the following year; when, after they had sent away their vessel, they discovered that their predecessor had been murdered, through the treachery of the renegade apostate; and they themselves fell shortly victims to his perfidy. Menendez dispatched a third vessel there; when the fate of the two former parties was ascertained, and he went in person to chastise the murderers; he succeeded in capturing six or seven,

PEDRO MENENDEZ DE AVILES

Founder of S.ᵗ Augustine 1565

who, it is said (rather improbably I think), confessed themselves to have been implicated in the massacre. Menendez, in his summary and sailor-like way, ordered their execution at the yard-arm of his vessel. The Cronicle says, that they were first converted and baptized, by the zeal of Father Rogel, before the sentence was carried into execution. A long period elapsed before any further efforts were made in this quarter to establish a colony; and it was then accomplished by the English. In consequence of these temporary establishments, however, the Spanish crown, for a long period, claimed the whole of the intervening country, as lying within its Province of Florida.

The annals of the city during the remainder of the life of Menendez, present only the usual vicissitudes of new settlements,—the alternations of supply and want, occasional disaffections, and petty annoyances.

Menendez was the recipient from his court of new honors from time to time, and had been appointed the grand admiral of the Spanish Armada; when, in September, 1574, he was suddenly carried off by a fever, at the age of fifty-five. It is a singular coincidence, that De Gourgues, five years afterwards, was carried off in a similar manner, just after his appointment as admiral of the French fleet. A splendid monument in the church of San Nicolas, at Aviles, was erected to the memory of Menendez, with the following inscription:

"HERE LIES BURIED THE ILLUSTRIOUS CAVALIER, PEDRO MENENDEZ DE AVILES, A NATIVE OF THIS CITY, ADELANTADO OF THE PROVINCES OF FLORIDA, KNIGHT COMMANDER OF SANTA CRUZ OF THE ORDER OF SANTIAGO, AND CAPTAIN GENERAL OF THE OCEANIC SEAS AND OF THE ARMADA WHICH HIS ROYAL HIGHNESS COLLECTED AT SANTANDER IN THE YEAR 1574, WHERE HE DIED ON THE 17TH OF SEPTEMBER OF THAT YEAR, IN THE 55TH YEAR OF HIS AGE.

CHAPTER XI.

SIR FRANCIS DRAKE'S ATTACK UPON ST. AUGUSTINE—ESTAB-
LISHMENT OF MISSIONS—MASSACRE OF MISSIONARIES AT
ST. AUGUSTINE—1586—1638.

NINE years had elapsed from the death of Menendez, and the colony at St. Augustine had slowly progressed into the settlement of a small town ; but the
eclat and importance which the presence of Menendez had given it, were much lessened ; when, in 1586,
Sir Francis Drake, with a fleet returning from South
America, discovered the Spanish look-out upon
Anastasia Island, and sent boats ashore to ascertain
something in reference to it. Marching up the shore,
they discovered across the bay, a fort, and further
up a town built of wood.

Proceeding towards the fort, which bore the name
of San Juan de Pinas, some guns were fired upon
them from it, and they retired towards their vessel ;
the same evening a fifer made his appearance, and
informed them that he was a Frenchman, detained
a prisoner there, and that the Spaniards had abandoned their fort ; and he offered to conduct them

over. Upon this information they crossed the river and found the fort abandoned as they had been informed, and took possession of it without opposition. It was built entirely of wood, and only surrounded by a wall or pale formed of the bodies or trunks of large trees, set upright in the earth; for, says the narrative, it was not at that time inclosed by a ditch, as it had been but lately begun by the Spaniards. The platforms were made of the bodies of large pine trees (of which there are plenty here), laid horizontally across each other, with earth rammed in to fill up the vacancies. Fourteen brass cannon were found in the fort, and there was left behind the treasure chest, containing £2,000 sterling, designed for the payment of the garrison, which consisted of one hundred and fifty men. Whether the massive, iron-bound mahogany chest, still preserved in the old fort is the same which fell into the hands of Drake, is a question for antiquaries to decide; its ancient appearance might well justify the supposition.

On the following day, Drake's forces marched towards the town, but owing, it is said, to heavy rains, were obliged to return and go in the boats. On their approach, the Spaniards fled into the country. It is said, in Barcia, that a Spaniard concealed in the bushes, fired at the sergeant major and wounded him, and then ran up and dispatched him, and that in revenge for this act, Drake burnt their buildings and destroyed their gardens. The garrison and inhabitants retired to fort San Matteo, on the St. Johns river. Barcia says that the population of the place was then increasing considerably, and that it possessed a hall of justice, parochial church, and other buildings, together with gardens in the rear of the town:

An engraved plan or view of Drake's descent upon St. Augustine, published after his return to England, represents an octagonal fort between two streams; at the distance of half a mile another stream; beyond that the town, with a look-out and two religious houses, one of which is a church and the other probably the house of the Franciscans, who had shortly before established a house of their order there. The town contains three squares lengthwise, and four in width, with gardens on the west side.

Some doubt has been thrown on the actual site of the first settlement, by this account; but I think it probably stood considerably to the south of the present public square, between the barracks and the powder-house. Perhaps the Maria Sanchez creek may have then communicated with the bay near its present head, in wet weather and at high tides isolating the fort from the town. The present north ditch may have been the bed of a tide creek, and thus would correspond to the appearance presented by the sketch. It is well known that the north end of ne city was built at a much later period than the southern, and that the now vacant space below the barracks, was once occupied with buildings. Buildings and fields are shown upon Anastasia Island, opposite the town. The relative position of the town with reference to the entrance of the harbor is correctly shown on the plan; and there seems no sufficient ground to doubt the identity of the present town with the ancient locality.

The garrison and country were then under the command of Don Pedro Menendez, a nephew of the Adelantado; who, after the English squadron sailed, having received assistance from Havana, began, it is said, to rebuild the city, and made great efforts to increase its population, and to induce the Indians to settle in its neighborhood.

In 1592, twelve Franciscan missionaries arrived at St. Augustine, with their Superior, Fray Jean de Silva, and placed themselves under the charge of Father Francis Manon, Warden of the convent of St. Helena. One of them, a Mexican, Father Francis Panja, drew up in the language of the Yemasees his "Abridgment of Christian Doctrine," said to be the first work compiled in any of our Indian languages.

The Franciscan Father Corpa, established a Mission house for the Indians at Talomato, in the northwest portion of the city of St. Augustine, where there was then an Indian village. Father Blas de Rodriguez, also called Montes, had an Indian Church at a village of the Indians, called Tapoqui, situated on the creek called Cano de la Leche, north of the fort ; and the church bearing the name of " Our Lady of the Milk " was situated on the elevated ground a quarter of a mile north of the fort, near the creek. A stone church existed at this locality as late as 1795, and the crucifix belonging to it is preserved in the Roman Catholic Church at St. Augustine.

These missions proceeded with considerable apparent success, large numbers of the Indians being received and instructed both at this and other missions.

Among the converts at the mission of Talomato, was the son of the cacique of the province of Guale, a proud and high-spirited young leader, who by no means submitted to the requirements of his spiritual fathers, but indulged in excesses which scandalized his profession. Father Corpa, after trying private remonstrances and warnings in vain, thought it necessary to administer to him a public rebuke. This aroused the pride of the young chief, and he suddenly left the mission, determined upon revenge. He gathered from the interior a band of warriors, whom he inspired with his own hatred against the missionaries. Returning to Talomato with his followers under the cover of night, he crept up to the mission house, burst open the chapel doors, and slew the devoted Father Corpa while at prayer; then severed his head from his body, set it upon a pike-staff, and threw his body out into the forest where it could never afterwards be found. The scene of this tragedy was in the neighborhood of the present Roman Catholic cemetery of St. Augustine.

As soon as this occurrence became known in the Indian village, all was excitement; some of the most devoted bewailing the death of their spiritual father, while others dreaded the consequences of so rash an act, and shrunk with terror from the vengeance of the Spaniards, which they foresaw would soon follow. The young chief of Guale gathered them around him, and in earnest tones addressed them. "Yes," said he, "the friar is dead. It would not have been done, if he would have allowed us to live as we did before we became Christians. We desire to return to our ancient customs; and we must provide for our defense against the punishment which will be hurled upon us by the Governor of Florida, which, if it be allowed to reach us, will be as rigorous for this single friar, as if we had killed them all. For the same power which we possess to destroy this one priest, we have to destroy them all."

His followers approved of what had been done, and said there was no doubt but that the same vengeance would fall upon them for the death of the one, as for all.

He then resumed. " Since we shall receive equal punishment for the death of this one, as though we had killed them all, let us regain the liberty of which these friars have robbed us, with their promises of good things which we have not yet seen, but which they seek to keep us in hope of, while they accumulate upon us who are called Christians, injuries and disgusts, making us quit our wives, restricting us to one only, and prohibiting us from changing her. They prevent us from having our balls, banquets, feasts, celebrations, games, and contests, so that being deprived of them, we lose our ancient valor and skill which we inherited from our ancestors. Although they oppress us with labor, refusing to grant even the respite of a few days, and although we are disposed to do all they require from us, they are not satisfied ; but for everything they reprimand us, injuriously treat us, oppress us, lecture us, call us bad Christians, and deprive us of all the pleasures which our fathers enjoyed, in the hope that they would give us heaven; by these frauds subjecting us and holding us under their absolute control. And what have we to hope except to be made slaves? If we now put them all to death, we shall destroy these excrescenses, and force the governor to treat us well."

The majority were carried away by his address, and rung out the war-cry of death and defiance. While still eager for blood, their chief led them to the Indian town of Tapoqui, the mission of Father Montes, on the Cano de la Leche; tumultuously rushing in, they informed the missionary of the fate of Father Corpa, and that they sought his own life and those of all his order; and then with uplifted weapons bade him prepare to die. He reasoned and remonstrated with them, portraying the folly and wickedness of their intentions, that the vengeance of the Spaniards would surely overtake them, and implored them with tears, that for their own sakes rather than his, they should pause in their mad designs. But all in vain; they were alike insensible to his eloquence, and his tears, and pressed forward to surround him. Finding all else vain, he begged as a last favor that he should be permitted to celebrate mass before he died. In this he was probably actuated in part by the hope that their fierce hatred might be assuaged by the sight of the ceremonies of their faith, or that the delay might afford time for succor from the adjoining garrison.

The permission was given; and there for the last time the worthy Father put on his robes, which might well be termed his robes of sacrifice. The wild and savage crowd, thirsting for his blood, reclined upon the floor and looked on in sullen silence, awaiting the conclusion of the rites. The priest alone, standing before the altar, proceeded with this most sad and solemn mass, then cast his eyes to heaven and knelt in private supplication; where the next moment he fell under the blows of his cruel foes, bespattering the altar at which he ministered, with his own life's blood. His crushed remains were thrown into the fields, that they might serve for the fowls of the air or the beasts of the forest; but not one would approach it, except a dog, which, rushing forward to lay hold upon the body, fell dead upon the spot, says the ancient chronicle; and an old Christian Indian, recognizing it, gave it sepulture in the forest.

From thence the ferocious young chief of Guale, led his followers against several missions, in other parts of the country, which he attacked and destroyed, together with their attendant clergy. Thus upon the soil of the ancient city, was shed the blood of Christian martyrs, who were laboring with a zeal well worthy of emulation, to carry the truths of religion to the native tribes of Florida. Two hundred and sixty years have passed away since these sad scenes were enacted; but we cannot even now repress a tear of sympathy and a feeling of admiration for those self-denying missionaries of the cross, who sealed their faith with their blood, and fell victims to their energy and devotion. The spectacle of the dying priest struck down at the altar, attired in his sacred vestments, and perhaps imploring pardon upon his murderers, cannot fail to call up in the heart of the most insensible, something more than a passing emotion.

The zeal of the Franciscans was only increased by this disaster, and each succeeding year brought additions to their number. They pushed their missions into the interior of the country so rapidly that in less than two years they had established through the principal towns of the Indians, no less than twenty mission houses. The presumed remains of these establishments are still occasionally to be found throughout the interior of the country.

CHAPTER XII.

SUBJECTION OF THE APALACHIAN. INDIANS—CONSTRUCTION
OF THE FORT, SEA WALL, &c.—1638—1700.

In the year 1638, hostilities were entered into
between the Spanish settlements on the coast, and
the Apalachian Indians, who occupied the country
in the neighborhood of the river Suwanee. The
Spaniards soon succeeded in subduing their Indian
foes; and in 1640, large numbers of the Apalachian
Indians were brought to St. Augustine, and in
alleged punishment for their outbreak, and with a
sagacious eye to the convenience of the arrangement,
were forced to labor upon the public works and fortifications of the city. At this period the English
settlements along the coast to the northward, had
begun to be formed, much to the uneasiness and
displeasure of the Spanish crown, which for a long
period claimed, by virtue of exploration and occupation, as well as by the ancient papal grant of
Alexander, all the eastern coast of the United
States. Their missionaries had penetrated Virginia

9

before the settlement at Jamestown; and they had built a fort in South Carolina, and kept up a garrison for some years in it. But the Spanish government had become too feeble to compete with either the English or the French on the seas; and with the loss of their celebrated Armada, perished for ever their pretensions as a naval power. They were therefore forced to look to the safety of their already established settlements in Florida; and the easy capture of the fort at St. Augustine by the passing squadron of Drake, evinced the necessity of works of a much more formidable character.

It is evident that the fort, or castle as it was usually designated, had been then commenced, although its form was afterwards changed; and for sixty years subsequently, these unfortunate Apalachian Indians were compelled to labor upon the works, until in 1680, upon the recommendation of their mission Fathers, they were relieved from further compulsory labor, with the understanding that in case of necessity they would resume their labors.

In 1648, St. Augustine is described to have contained more than three hundred householders (*vecinos*), a flourishing monastery of the order of St. Francis with fifty Franciscans, men very zealous for the conversion of the Indians, and regarded by their countrymen with the highest veneration. Besides these there were in the city alone, a vicar, a parochial curate, a superior sacristan, and a chaplain attached to the castle. The parish church was built of wood, the Bishop of Cuba, it is said, not being able to afford anything better, his whole income being but four hundred pezos per annum, which he shared with Florida; and sometimes he expended much more than his receipts.

In 1665, Captain Davis, one of the English buccaneers and freebooters (then very numerous in the West Indies), with a fleet of seven or eight vessels came on the coast from Jamaica, to intercept the Spanish plate fleet on its return from New Spain to Europe; but being disappointed in this scheme, he proceeded along the coast of Florida, and came off St. Augustine, where he landed and marched directly upon the town, which he sacked and plundered, without meeting the least opposition or resistance from the Spaniards, although they had then a garrison of two hundred men in the fort, which at that time was an octagon, fortified and defended by round towers.

The fortifications, if this account be true, were probably then very incomplete; and with a vastly inferior force it is not surprising that they did not undertake what could only have been an ineffectual resistance. It does not appear that the fort was taken; and the inhabitants retired probably within its inclosure with their valuables.*

In the Spanish account of the various occurrences in this country, it is mentioned that in 1681, "the English having examined a province of Florida, distant twelve leagues from another called New Castle, where the air is pleasant, the climate mild, and the lands very fertile, called it Silvania; and that knowing these advantages, a Quaker, or Shaker (a sect barbarous, impudent, and abominable), called William Penn, obtained a grant of it from Charles II., King of England, and made great efforts to colonize it." Such was the extent then claimed for the province of Florida, and such the opinion entertained of the Quakers.

In 1681, Don Juan Marquez Cabrera, applied himself at once, upon his appointment to the govership of Florida, to finishing the castle; and collected large quantities of stone, lime, timber, and iron, more than sufficient subsequently to complete it. About this period, a new impulse was given to the extension of the missions for converting the Indians; and large reinforcements of the clerical force were received from Mexico, Havana, and Spain; and many

---

* I do not find any account of this expedition and capture of St. Augustine in the Ensayo Cronologica.

of them received salaries from the crown. A considerable Indian town is spoken of at this period, as existing six hundred varas north of St. Augustine, and called Macarasi, which would correspond to the place formerly occupied by Judge Douglas (where, in Multicaulis' times, he built a cocoonery), and which has long been called Macariz. Other parts of the country were known by various names. Amelia Island was the province of Guale. The southern part of the country was known as the province of Carlos. Indian River was the province of Ys. Westwardly was the province of Apalachie; while smaller divisions were designated by the names of the chiefs.

It is hardly to be doubted, that the same spirit of oppression towards the Indians, exercised in the other colonies under Spanish domination, existed in Florida. It has been already mentioned that the Apalachians were kept at labor upon the fortifications of St. Augustine; and in 1680, the Yemasees, who had always been particularly peaceful and manageable, and whose principal town was Macarisqui, near St. Augustine, revolted at the rule exercised over them by the Spanish authorities at St. Augustine, in consequence of the execution of one of their chiefs by the order of the governor; and six years afterwards they made a general attack upon the Spaniards, drove them within the walls of the castle, and became such mortal enemies to them, that they never gave a Spaniard quarter, waylaying, and invariably massacring, any stragglers they could intercept outside of the fort.

In 1670, an English settlement was established near Port Royal, South Carolina, one hundred and five years subsequent to the settlement of St. Augustine. The Spaniards regarded it as an infringement upon their rights; and although a treaty, after this settlement, had been made between Spain and England, confirming to the latter all her settlements and islands, yet as no boundaries or limits were mentioned, their respective rights and boundaries remained a subject of dispute for seventy years.

About 1675, the Spanish authorities at St. Augustine, having intelligence from *white servants* who fled to them, of the discontented and miserable situation of the colony in Carolina, advanced with a party under arms as far as the island of St. Helena, to dislodge or destroy the settlers. A treacherous colonist of the name of Fitzpatrick, deserted to the Spaniards; but the governor, Sir John Yeamans, having received a reinforcement, held his ground; and a detachment of fifty volunteers under Colonel Godfrey, marched against the enemy, forcing them

to retire from the Island of St. Helena, and retreat
to St. Augustine.*

Ten years afterwards, three galleys sailed from St.
Augustine, and attacked a Scotch and English settlement at Port Royal, which had been founded by
Lord Cardross, in 1681. The settlement was weak
and unprotected, and the Spaniards fell upon them,
killing several, whipped many, plundered all, and
broke up the colony. Flushed with success, they
continued their depredations on Edisto River, burning the houses, wasting the plantations, and robbing
the settlers ; and finished their marauding expedition
by capturing the brother of Governor Morton, and
burning him alive in one of the galleys which a
hurricane had driven so high upon land as to make
it impossible to have it re-launched. Such at least is
the English account of the matter ; and they say that
intestine troubles alone prevented immediate and signal retaliation by the South Carolinians.†

One captain Don Juan de Aila, went to Spain in
the year 1687, in his own vessel, to procure additional
forces and ammunition for the garrison at St. Augustine. He received the men and munitions desired ;

---

* Carroll's S. C., Vol. 1, p. 62.

† Rivers' S. C. Hist. Coll. p. 143. Do. Appendix, 425. Carroll's Coll.,
2d vol., 350.

and as a reward for his diligence and patriotism, he also received the privilege of carrying merchandise, duty free; being also allowed to take twelve Spanish negroes for the cultivation of the fields of Florida, of whom it is said there was a great want in that province. By a mischance, he was only able to carry one negro there, with the troops and other cargo, and was received in the city with universal joy. This was the first occasion of the reception of African slaves; although as has been heretofore mentioned, it was made a part of the royal stipulation with Menendez, that he should bring over five hundred negro slaves.

Don Diego de Quiroga y Losada, the governor of Florida in 1690, finding that the sea was making dangerous encroachments upon the shores of the town, and had reached even the houses, threatening to swallow them up, and render useless the fort which had cost so much to put in the state of completion in which it then was, called a public meeting of the chief men and citizens of the place, and proposed to them that in order to escape the danger which menaced them, and to restrain the force of the sea, they should construct a wall, which should run from the castle and cover and protect the city from all danger of the sea. The inhabitants not only approved of his proposal, but began the work with so much zeal, that the soldiers gave more than seventeen hundred dollars of their wages, although they were very much behind, not having been paid in six years; with which the governor began to make the necessary preparations, and sent forward a dispatch to the home government upon the subject.

The council of war of the Indies approved, in the following year, of the work of the sea wall, and directed the viceroy of New Spain to furnish ten thousand dollars for it, and directed that a plan and estimate of the work should be forwarded. Quiroga was succeeded in the governorship of Florida, by Don Laureano de Torres, who went forward with the work of the sea wall, and received for this purpose the means furnished by the soldiers, and one thousand dollars more, which they offered besides the two thousand dollars, and likewise six thousand dollars which had come from New Spain, remitted by the viceroy, Count de Galleo, for the purpose of building a tower, as a look-out to observe the surrounding Indian settlements. Whether this tower was erected, or where, we have no certain knowledge. The towers erected on the governor's palace and at the northeast angle of the fort, were intended as look-outs both sea and landward.

The statements made in reference to the building of this wall, from the castle as far as the city, confirms the opinion previously expressed, that the ancient and early settlement of the place was south of the public square, as the remains of the ancient sea wall extend to the basin at the Plaza. The top of this old sea wall is still visible along the center of Bay street, where it occasionally appears above the level of the street; and its general plan and arrangement are shown on several old maps and plans of the city. Upon a plan of the city made in 1665, it is represented as terminating in a species of break-water at the public square. It is unnecessary to add that the present sea wall is a much superior structure to the old, and extends above twice the distance. Its cost is said to have been one hundred thousand dollars, and it was building from 1837 to 1843.

In the year 1700, the work on the sea wall had progressed but slowly, although the governor had employed thirty stone-cutters at a time, and had eight yoke of oxen drawing stone to the landing, and two lime-kilns all the while at work. But the money previously provided, and considerable additional funds was requisite, resembling in this respect its successor. The new governor, De Cuniza, took the matter in hand, as he had much experience in fortifications. The defenses of the fort are spoken of as being at the time too weak to resist artillery, and the sea wall as being but a slight work.

CHAPTER XIII.

ATTACK ON ST. AUGUSTINE BY GOV. MOORE OF SOUTH CAR-
OLINA—DIFFICULTIES WITH THE GEORGIANS.—1702—1732.

HOSTILITIES had broken out between England and
Spain in 1702. The English settlements in Carolina
only numbered six or seven thousand inhabitants,
when Gov. Moore, who was an ambitious and energetic man, but with serious defects of character, led
an invading force from Carolina against St. Augustine. The pretense was to retaliate for old injuries,
and, by taking the initiative, to prevent an attack
upon themselves. The real motive was said by
Gov. Moore's opponents at home, to have been the
acquisition of military reputation and private gain.

The plan of the expedition embraced a combined
land and naval attack ; and for this purpose six
hundred provincial militia were embodied, with an
equal number of Indian allies ; a portion of the
militia, with the Indians, were to go inland by boats
and by land, under the command of Col. Daniel,

who is spoken of as a good officer, while the main body proceeded with the governor by sea in several merchant schooners and ships which had been impressed for the service.

The Spaniards, who had received intimations of the contemplated attack, placed themselves in the best posture of defense in their power, and laid up provisions in the castle to withstand a long siege.

The forces under Col. Daniel arrived in advance of the naval fleet of the expedition, and immediately marched upon the town. The inhabitants, upon his approach, retired with their most valuable effects within the spacious walls of the castle, and Col. Daniel entered and took possession of the town, the larger part of which, it must be recollected, was at some distance from the castle.

The quaint description of these events, given by Oldmixon, is as follows :—

" Col. Rob. Daniel, a very brave man, commanded a party who were to go up the river in periagas, and come upon Augustino on the land side, while the Governour sailed thither, and attacked it by sea. They both set out in August, 1702. Col. Daniel, in his way, took St. Johns, a small Spanish settlement; as also St. Mary's, another little village belonging to the Spaniards; after which he proceeded to Augustino, came before the town, entered and took it, Col. Moor not being yet arrived with the fleet.

" The inhabitants having notice of the approach of the English, had packed up their best effects and retired with them into the castle, which was surrounded by a very deep and broad moat.

" They had laid up provisions there for four months, and resolved to defend themselves to the last extremity. However, Col. Daniel found a considerable booty in the town. The next day the Governour came ashore, and his troops following him, they entrenched, posted their guards in the church, and blocked up the castle. The English held possession of the town a whole month; but finding they could do nothing for want of mortars and bombs, they despatched away a sloop for Jamaica; but the commander of the sloop, instead of going thither, came to Carolina out of fear of treachery. Finding others offered to go in his stead, he proceeded in the voyage himself, after he had lain some time at Charlestown.

" The Governour all this while lay before the castle of Augustino, in expectation of the return of the sloop, which hearing nothing of, he sent Col. Daniel, who was the life of the action, to Jamaica on the same errand.

This gentleman, being hearty in the design, procured a supply of bombs, and returned towards Augustino. But in the mean time two ships appeared in the offing, which being taken to be two very large men of war, the Governour thought fit to raise the siege and abandon his ships, with a great quantity of stores, ammunition, and provision, to the enemy. Upon which the two men of war entered the port of Augustino, and took the Governour's ships. Some say he burnt them himself. Certain it is they were lost to the English, and that he returned to Charles-Town over land 300 miles from Augustino. The two men of war that were thought to be so large, proved to be two small frigates, one of 82, and the other of 16 guns.*

" When Col. Daniel came back to St. Augustino, he was chased, but got away; and Col. Moor retreated with no great honor homewards. The periagas lay at St. Johns, whither the Governour retired and so to Charles-Town, having lost but two men in the whole expedition."

Arratomakaw, king of the Yamioseans, who commanded the Indians, retreated to the periagas with the rest, and there slept upon his oars with a great deal of bravery and unconcern. The gover-

---

* There must be an error, of course, in this statement of an 82-gun ship entering St. Augustine, as the depth of water would never admit a vessel of over 300 tons: probably 82 should read 12 guns.   G. R. F.

nor's soldiers, taking a false alarm, and thinking the Spaniards were coming, did not like this slow pace of the Indian king in his flight, and to quicken him into it, bade him make more haste. But he replied, "No; though your governor leaves you, I will not stir till I have seen all my men before me."

The Spanish accounts say that he burned the town, and this statement is confirmed by the report made on the 18th July, 1740, by a committee of the House of Commons of the province of South Carolina, in which it is said, referring to these transactions, that Moore was obliged to retreat, *but not without* first burning the town.*

It seems that the plunder carried off by Moore's troops was considerable; as his enemies charged at the time that he sent off a sloop-load to Jamaica, and in an old colonial document of South Carolina, it is represented "that the late unfortunate, ill-contrived, and worse managed expedition against St. Augustine, was principally set on foot by the said late governor and his adherents; and that if any person in the said late assembly undertook to speak against it, and to show how unfit and unable we were at that time for such an attempt, he was presently looked upon by them as an enemy

---

* Carroll's Hist. Coll., vol. 2, p. 352.

and traitor to his country, and reviled and affronted in the said assembly; although the true design of the said expedition was no other than catching and making slaves of Indians for private advantage, and impoverishing the country. * * * And that the expedition was to enrich themselves will appear particularly, because whatsoever booty, as rich silks, great quantity of church plate, with a great many other costly church ornaments and utensils taken by our soldiers at St. Augustine, are now detained in the possession of the said late governor and his officers, contrary to an act of assembly made for an equal division of the same amongst the soldiers." *

The Spanish accounts of this expedition of Moore's are very meager. They designate him as the governor of St. George, by which name they called the harbor of Charleston; and they also speak of the plunder of the town, and the burning of the greater part of the houses. Don Joseph de Curriga was the then governor of the city, and had received just previous to the English attack, reinforcements from Havana, and had repaired and strengthened the fortifications.

The retreat of the English was celebrated with great rejoicing by the Spaniards, who had been for

---

* Rivers' Hist. Sketches. S. C., app. 456.

three months shut up within the limited space of the walls of the castle; and they gladly repaired their ruined homes, and made good the ravages of the English invasion. An English account says that the two vessels which appeared off the bar and caused Moore's precipitate retreat, contained but two hundred men, and that had he awaited Colonel Daniel's return with the siege guns and ammunition, the castle would have fallen into their hands.

In the same year, the king of Spain, alarmed at the dangers which menaced his possessions in Florida, gave greater attention to the strengthening the defenses of St. Augustine, and forwarded considerable reinforcements to the garrison, as well as additional supplies of munitions.

The works were directed to be strengthened, which Governor Curriga thought not as strong as had been represented, and that the sea wall in the process of erection, was insufficient for the purpose for which it was designed.

Sixty years had elapsed since the Apalachian Indians had been conquered and compelled to labor upon the fortifications of St. Augustine; their chiefs now asked that they might be relieved from further compulsory labor; and after the usual number of references and reports and informations, through the Spanish circumlocution offices, this was graciously

10

granted in a suspensory form, until their services should be again required.

During the year 1712, a great scarcity of provisions, caused by the failure of the usual supply vessels, reduced the inhabitants of St. Augustine to the verge of starvation; and, for two or three months, they were obliged to live upon horses, cats, dogs, and other disgusting animals. It seems strange, that after a settlement of nearly one hundred and fifty years, the Spaniards in Florida should still be dependent upon the importation of provisions for their support; and that anything like the distress indicated should prevail, with the abundant resources they had, from the fish, oysters, turtle, and clams of the sea, and the arrow-root and cabbage-tree palm of the land.

The English settlements were now extending into the interior portions of South Carolina; and the French had renewed their efforts at settlement and colonization upon the rivers discharging into the Gulf of Mexico. All three nations were competitors for the trade with the Indians, and kept up an intriguing rivalship for this trade for more than a hundred years.

There seems to have been at this period, a policy pursued by the Spanish authorities in Florida, of the most reprehensible character. The strongest efforts were made to attach all the Indian tribes to the Spanish interest; and they were encouraged to carry on a system of plunder and annoyance upon the English settlements of Carolina. They particularly seized upon all the negroes they could obtain, and carried them to the governor at St. Augustine; who invariably refused to surrender them, alleging that he was acting under the instructions of his government in so doing.

In 1704, Governor Moore had made a sweeping and vigorous excursion against the Indian towns in Middle Florida, all of whom were in the Spanish interest; and had broken up and destroyed the towns, and missions attached to them. In 1725, Colonel Palmer determined, since no satisfaction could be obtained for the incursions of the Spanish Indians, and the loss of their slaves, to make a descent upon them; and with a party of three hundred men entered Florida, with an intention of visiting upon the province all the desolation of retributive warfare.

He went up to the very gates of St. Augustine, and compelled the inhabitants to seek protection within the castle. In his course he swept every thing before him, destroying every house, field, and improvement within his reach; carrying off the live-stock, and every thing else of value. The

Spanish Indians who fell within his power, were slain in large numbers, and many were taken prisoners. Outside of the walls of St. Augustine nothing was left undestroyed; and the Spanish authorities received a memorable lesson in the law of retribution.

CHAPTER XIV.

SIEGE OF ST. AUGUSTINE, BY OGLETHORPE.—1732—1740.

DIFFICULTIES existed for many years subsequently, between the Spanish and English settlements. In 1732, Oglethorpe planted his colony in Georgia, and extended his settlements along the coast towards Florida, claiming and occupying the country up to the margin of the St. Johns, and established a post at St. George Island. This was deemed an invasion of the territory of Spain; and the post was attacked unfairly, as the English say, and some of their men murdered. Oglethorpe, upon this, acting under the instructions of the home government, commenced hostilities, by arranging a joint attack, of the forces of South Carolina and Georgia, with a view to the entire conquest of Florida.

The instructions of the king of England to Oglethorpe, were, that he should make a naval and land attack upon St. Augustine; "and if it shall please God to give you success, you are either to demolish the fort and bastions, or put a garrison in it, in case you shall have men enough for that purpose; which last, it is thought, will be the best way to prevent the Spaniards from endeavoring to retake and settle the said place again, at any time hereafter." *

Don Manuel Monteano was then governor of Florida, and in command of the garrison. The city and castle were previously in a poor condition to withstand an attack from a well-prepared foe; and on the 11th November, 1737, Governor Monteano writes to the governor-general of Cuba, that "the fort of this place is its only defense; it has no casemates for the shelter of the men, nor the necessary elevation to the counter-scarp, nor covert ways, nor ravelins to the curtains, nor other exterior works that could give time for a long defense; but it is thus naked outside, as it is without soul within, for there are no cannon that could be fired twenty-four hours, and though there were, artillery-men to manage them are wanting."

Under the superintendence of an able officer of engineers, Don Antonio de Arredando, the works were put in order; the ramparts were heightened and casemated; a covered way was made, by planting and embanking four thousand stakes; bombproof vaults were constructed, and entrenchments

---

* State Papers of Georgia.   Ga. Hist. Soc.

thrown up around the town, protected by ten salient angles, many of which are still visible. The garrison of the town was about seven hundred and forty soldiers, according to Governor Monteano's return of troops. On the 25th March, 1740, the total population of St. Augustine, of all classes, was two thousand one hundred and forty-three.

Previous to his attack upon the place, General Oglethorpe obtained the following information from prisoners whom he took at the outposts. He says, "They agree that there are fifty pieces of cannon in the castle at St. Augustine, several of which are of brass, from twelve to forty-eight pounds. It has four bastions. The walls are of stone, and casemated. The internal square is sixty yards. The ditch is forty feet wide, and twelve feet deep, six of which is sometimes filled with water. The counterscarp is faced with stone. They have lately made a covered way. The town is fortified with an entrenchment, salient angles, and redoubts, which inclose about half a mile in length, and a quarter of a mile in width. The inhabitants and garrison, men, women, and children, amount to above two thousand five hundred. For the garrison, the king pays eight companies, sent from Spain two years since for the invasion of Georgia; upon establishment fifty-three men each, three companies of foot and one of artillery, of the old garrison, and one troop of horse one hundred each upon establishment; of these, one hundred are at St. Marks, ten days' march from St. Augustine; upon the Gulf of Mexico, one hundred are disposed in several small forts."

Of these out-posts, there were two, one on each side of the river St. Johns—at Picolata, and immediately opposite—and at Diego. The purpose of the forts at Picolata was to guard the passage of the river, and to keep open the communication with St. Marks and Pensacola; and when threatened with the invasion of Oglethorpe, messengers were dispatched to the governor of Pensacola for aid, and also to Mexico by the same route. The fort at Diego was but a small work, erected by Don Diego de Spinosa, upon his own estate; and the remains of it, with one or two cannon, are still visible. Fort Moosa was an out-post at the place now known by that name, on the North River, about two miles north of St. Augustine. A fortified line, a considerable portion of which may be now traced, extended across from the stoccades on the St. Sebastian, to Fort Moosa; a communication by a tide creek existed through the marshes, between the castle at St. Augustine and Fort Moosa.

Oglethorpe first attacked the two forts at Picolata, one of which, called Fort Pappa, or St. Francis de

Pappa, was a place of some strength. Its remains still exist, about one-fourth of a mile north of the termination of the Bellamy Road, its earthworks being still strongly marked.

After a slight resistance, both forts fell into his hands, much to the annoyance of Governor Monteano. Oglethorpe speaks of Fort Francis as being of much importance, "as commanding the passes from St. Augustine to Mexico, and into the country of the Creek Indians, and also being upon the ferry, where the troops which come from St. Augustine must pass." He found in it, one mortar piece, two carriages, three small guns, ammunition, one hundred and fifty shells, and fifty glass bottles full of gunpowder, with fuses—a somewhat novel missile of war.

The English general's plan of operation was, that the crews and troops upon the vessels should land, and throw up batteries upon Anastasia Island, from thence bombarding the town; while he himself, designed to lead the attack on the land side. Having arrived in position, he gave the signal of attack to the fleet, by sending up a rocket; but no response came from the vessels, and he had the mortification of being obliged to withdraw his troops. The troops were unable to effect a landing from the vessels, in consequence of a number of armed Spanish galleys having been drawn up inside the bar; so that no landing could be made except under a severe fire, while the galleys were protected from an attack by the ships, in consequence of the shoal water.

He then prepared to reduce the town by a regular siege, with a strict blockade by sea. He hoped, by driving the inhabitants into the castle, so to encumber the governor with useless mouths, as to reduce him to the necessity of a surrender to avoid starvation. The town was placed under the range of his heavy artillery and mortars, and soon became untenable, forcing the citizens generally to seek the shelter of the fort.

Col. Vanderduysen was posted at Point Quartel; and others of the troops upon Anastasia Island, and the north beach. Three batteries were erected: one on Anastasia Island, called the Poza, which consisted of four eighteen-pounders and one nine-pounder; one on the point of the wood of the island, mounting two eighteen-pounders. The remains of the Poza battery are still to be seen, almost as distinctly marked as on the day of its erection. Four mortars and forty cohorns were employed in the siege.

The siege began on the 12th June; and on the 25th June a night sortie was made from the castle

against a portion of the troops under command of
Col. Palmer, who were encamped at Fort Moosa,
including a company of Scotch Highlanders, numbering eighty-five men, under their chief, Capt. McIntosh, all equipped in Highland dress. This attack was
entirely successful, and the English sustained a severe
loss, their colonel being killed, with twenty Highlanders, twenty-seven soldiers, and a number of Indians.

This affair at Fort Moosa has generally been considered as a surprise, and its disastrous results as the
consequence of carelessness and disobedience of the
orders of Oglethorpe. Captain McIntosh, the leader
of the Highlanders, was taken prisoner, and finally
transferred to Spain. From his prison at St. Sebastian, under date of 20th June, 1741, he gives the
following account of the matter :—

"I listed seventy men, all in Highland dress, and
marched to the siege, and was ordered to scout nigh
St. Augustine and molest the enemy, while the general and the rest of his little army went to an island
where we could have no succor of them. I punctu-
ally obeyed my orders, until seven hundred Spaniards sallied out from the garrison, an hour before
daylight. *They did not surprise us*, for we were all
under arms, ready to receive them, which we did
briskly, keeping a constant firing for a quarter of an
hour, when they prest on with numbers; was

obliged to take our swords until the most of us was shot and cut to pieces. You are to observe we had but eighty men ; and the engagement was in view of the rest of our army, but they could not come to our assistance, by being in the foresaid island, under the enemy's guns. They had twenty prisoners, a few got off, the rest killed ; as we were well informed by some of themselves, they had three hundred killed on the spot,* besides several wounded. We were all stripped naked of clothes, brought to St. Augustine, where we remained three months in close confinement.†

This officer was Capt. John McIntosh ; and his son, Brig. Gen. McIntosh, then a youth of fourteen, was present in the engagement, and escaped without injury. The family of the McIntoshes have always been conspicuous in the history of Georgia.

The large number of persons collected within the walls of the castle, and under the protection of its battlements, soon gave rise to serious apprehensions on the part of the besieged, of being reduced by starvation to the necessity of a speedy surrender.

---

* This statement is unsupported by either Spanish or English authority. The writer of the letter, through want of familiarity with their language, misunderstood his informants, in all probability, as to the extent of their loss.

† MSS. in Geo. Hist. Soc. Library.

The batteries of Oglethorpe were planted at so great a distance that he could produce but little effect by his shot or shells upon the castle, although he rendered the city itself untenable. The heat of the season and the exposure, to which the Provincial militia were unaccustomed, soon produced considerable sickness and discouragement in the invading force, and affected Oglethorpe himself.

The Spanish governor sent most urgent messages to the governor of the island of Cuba, which were transmitted by runners along the coast, and thence by small vessels across to Havana. In one of these letters he says, " My greatest anxiety is for provisions; and if they do not come, there is no doubt of our dying by the hands of hunger." In another, he says, " I assure your Lordship, that it is impossible to express the confusion of the place; for we have no protection except the fort, and all the rest is open field. The families have abandoned their houses, and come to put themselves under the guns, which is pitiable; though nothing gives me anxiety but the want of provisions; and if your Lordship for want competent force cannot send relief, we must all perish." *

With the exception of the Fort Moosa affair, the

* Monteano, MSS., Archives St. Augustine.

hostilities were confined to the exchange of shots between the castle and the batteries.   Considerable discrepancy exists between the Spanish and English accounts, as to the period when the garrison was relieved : it was the communication of the fact of relief having been received, which formed the ostensible ground of abandoning the siege by Oglethorpe ; but the Spanish governor asserts, that these provision vessels did not arrive until the siege was raised. The real fact, I am inclined to think, is that the provision vessels arrived at Mosquito, a harbor sixty miles below, where they were to await orders from Gov. Monteano, as to the mode of getting discharged,* and that the information of their arrival, being known at St. Augustine, was communicated to the English, and thus induced their raising the siege; in fact, the hope of starving out the garrison was the only hope left to Oglethorpe ; his strength was insufficient for an assault, and his means inadequate to reduce the castle, which was well manned and well provided with means of defense.

It was in truth a hopeless task, under the circumstances, for Oglethorpe to persevere; and it is no impeachment of his courage or his generalship, that he was unable to take a fortress of really very respectable strength.

---

* Monteano, MS. Letter of, 28th July, 1740.

The siege continued from the 13th June, to the 20th July, a period of thirty-eight days. The bombardment was kept up twenty days, but owing to the lightness of the guns and the long range, but little effect was produced on the strong walls of the castle. Its spongy, infrangible walls received the balls from the batteries like a cotton bale, or sand battery, almost without making an impression; this may be seen on examination, since the marks remain to this day, as they were left at the end of the siege, one hundred and seventeen years ago.

The prosecution of the siege having become impracticable, preparations were made for retiring; and Oglethorpe, as a pardonable and characteristic protest against the assumption of his acting from any coercion, with drums beating and banners displayed crossed over to the main land, and marched in full view of the castle, to his encampment three miles distant, situated probably at the point now known as Pass Navarro.

Great credit and respect have been deservedly awarded to Governor Monteano, for the courage, skill, and perseverance with which he sustained the siege.

It is well known that the English general, had in a few months, an ample opportunity of showing to his opponent, that his skill in defending his own territory under the most disadvantageous circum-

stances, was equal to that of the accomplished Monteano himself. The defense of Frederica, and signal
defeat of the Spanish forces at Fort Simons, will ever
challenge for Oglethorpe the highest credit for the
most sterling qualities of a good general and a great
man.

Two years subsequently, Oglethorpe again advanced into Florida, appeared before the gates of St.
Augustine, and endeavored to induce the garrison
to march out to meet him; but they kept within
their walls, and Oglethorpe in one of his dispatches
says, in the irritation caused by their prudence, "that
they were so meek there was no provoking them."
As in this incursion he had no object in view but a
devastation of the country, and harrassing the
enemy, he shortly withdrew his forces.

A committee of the South Carolina House of Commons, in a report upon the Oglethorpe expedition,
thus speaks of St. Augustine, evidently smarting
under the disappointment of their recent defeat.
"July 1st, 1741."

"St. Augustine, in the possession of the crown of
Spain, is well known to be situated but little distance from hence, in latitude thirty degrees, in Florida, the next territory to us. It is maintained by
his Catholic Majesty, partly to preserve his claim to
Florida, and partly that it may be of service to the
plate-fleets when coming through the gulf, by show-

ing lights to them along the coast, and by being ready to give assistance when any of them are cast away thereabout. The castle, by the largest account, doth not cover more than one acre of ground, but is allowed on all hands to be a place of great strength, and hath been usually garrisoned with about three or four hundred men of the king's regular troops. The town is not very large, and but indifferently fortified. The inhabitants, many of which are mulattoes of savage dispositions, are all in the king's pay; also being registered from their birth, and a severe penalty laid on any master of a vessel that shall attempt to carry any of them off. These are formed into a militia, and have been generally computed to be near about the same number as the regular troops. Thus relying wholly on the king's pay for their subsistence, their thoughts never turned to trade or even agriculture, but depending on foreign supplies for the most common necessaries of life, they spent their time in universal, perpetual idleness. From such a state, mischievous inclinations naturally sprung up in such a people; and having leisure and opportunity, ever since they had a neighbor the fruits of whose industry excited their desires and envy, they have not failed to carry those inclinations into action as often as they could, without the least regard to peace or war subsisting between the two crowns of Great Britain and Spain, or to

11

stipulations agreed upon between the two govern-
ments."*

Among the principal grievances set forth in this
report, was the carrying off and enticing and harbor-
ing their slaves, of which a number of instances are
enumerated; and they attributed the negro insurrection which occurred in South Carolina, in 1739, to
the connivance and agency of the Spanish authorities
at St. Augustine; and they proceed in a climax of
indignation to hurl their denunciation at the supposed authors of their misfortunes, in the following
terms: "With indignation we looked at St. Augustine (like another Sallee!) That den of thieves
and ruffians! receptacle of debtors, servants and
slaves! bane of industry and society! and revolved
in our minds all the injuries this province had received
from thence, ever since its first settlement. That
they had from first to last, in times of profoundest
peace, both publickly and privately, by themselves,
Indians, and Negroes, in every shape molested us, not
without some instances of uncommon cruelty."†

It is very certain there was on each side, enough
supposed causes of provocation to induce a far from
amiable state of feeling between these neighboring
colonies.

---

* Report upon Expedition to St. Augustine. Carroll's Coll. 2d vol.,
p. 354.

† Carroll's Hist. Coll. S. C., p. 359.

CHAPTER XV.

COMPLETION OF THE CASTLE—DESCRIPTIONS OF ST. AUGUS-
TINE A CENTURY AGO—ENGLISH OCCUPATION OF FLORIDA.
1755—1763—1783.

Don Alonzo Fernandez de Herrera was appointed
governor of Florida in 1755, and completed the
exterior works and finish of the fort.   It is this governor who erected the tablet over its main entrance,
with the Spanish coat of arms sculptured in alto
relievo, with the following inscription beneath :—

REYNANDO EN ESPANA EL SEN^R
DON FERNANDO SEXTO Y SIENDO
GOV^{OR} Y CAP^N DE ES^A C^D S^{AN} AUG^N DE
LA FLORIDA Y SUS PROV^A EL MARISCAL
DE CAMPO D^N ALONZO FERN^{DO} HEREDA
ASI CONCLUIO ESTE CASTILLO EL AN
OD 1756 DIRI^G_AENDO LAS OBRAS EL
CAP. INGN^{RO} DN PEDRO DE BROZAS
Y GARAY.

Don Ferdinand the Sixth, being king of Spain,
and the Field Marshal, Don Alonzo Fer-

NANDO HEREDA, BEING GOVERNOR AND CAPTAIN
GENERAL OF THIS PLACE, ST. AUGUSTINE, OF FLO-
RIDA, AND ITS PROVINCE. THIS FORT WAS FINISHED
IN THE YEAR 1756. THE WORKS WERE DIRECTED
BY THE CAPTAIN ENGINEER, DON PEDRO DE BRAZOS
Y GARAY.

I am not sure but that the boastful governor
might with equal propriety and truth, have put
a similar inscription at the city gate, claiming the
town also as a finished city.

The first fort erected was called San Juan de
Pinos, and probably the same name attached to the
present fort at the commencement of its erection;
when it acquired the name of St. Mark, I have not
discovered. The Apalachian Indians were employed
upon it for more than sixty years, and to their efforts
are probably due the evidences of immense labor in
the construction of the ditch, the ramparts and glacis,
and the approaches; while the huge mass of stone
contained in its solid walls, must have required the
labor of hundreds of persons for many long years,
in procuring and cutting the stone in the quarries on
the island, transporting it to the water, and across
the bay, and fashioning and raising them to their
places. Besides the Indians employed, some labor
was constantly bestowed by the garrison; and for
a considerable period, convicts were brought hither

from Mexico to carry on the public works. During
the works of extension and repair effected by Monteano, previous to the siege by Oglethorpe, he employed upon it one hundred and forty of these
Mexican convicts. The southwestern bastion is said
to have been completed by Monteano. The bastions
bore the names respectively of St. Paul, St. Peter,
St. James, &c.

The whole work remains now as it was in 1756,
with the exception of the water battery, which was
reconstructed by the government of the United
States in 1842-3. The complement of its guns is
one hundred, and its full garrison establishment
requires one thousand men. It is built upon the
plan of Vauban, and is considered by military men
as a very creditable work; its strength and efficiency
have been well tested in the old times; for it has
never been taken, although twice besieged, and
several times attacked. Its frowning battlements
and sepulchral vaults, will long stand after we and
those of our day shall be numbered with that long
past, of which it is itself a memorial; of its legends
connected with the dark chambers and prison vaults,
the chains, the instruments of torture, the skeletons
walled in, its closed and hidden recesses—of Coa-
couchee's escape, and many another tale, there is much
to say ; but it is better said within its grim walls,

where the eye and the imagination can go together, in weaving a web of mystery and awe over its sad associations, to the music of the grating bolt, the echoing tread, and the clanking chain.

Of the city itself, we have the following description in 1754 :—

"It is built on a little bay, at the foot of a hill shaded by trees, and forms an oblong square, divided into four streets, and has two full streets, which cut each other at right angles. The houses are well built, and regular. They have only one church, which is called after the city. St. John's Fort, standing about a mile north of it, is a strong, irregular fortification, well mounted with cannon, and capable of making a long defense."

I am inclined to think that the *mile* between the fort and the city, and the *hill* at the foot of which, he says, the city was built, existed only in the focus of the writer's spectacles.

The Provinces of Florida were ceded by treaty to England in the year 1763, and the Spanish inhabitants very generally left the country, which had then been under Spanish rule for near two hundred years ; and certainly in no portion of this country, had less progress been made. Beyond the walls occupied by its garrison, little had been attempted or accomplished in these two hundred years. This was in part, perhaps, attributable to the circumstances of the country,—the frequent hostility of the Indians, and the want of that mutual support given by neighborhoods, which in Florida are less practicable than elsewhere; but it was still more owing to the character of the Spanish inhabitants, who were more soldiers than civilians, and more townsmen than agriculturists; at all events, at the cession of Florida to Great Britain, the number of inhabitants was not over five thousand.

Of the period of the English occupation of Florida, we have very full accounts. It was a primary object with the British government, to colonize and settle it; and inducements to emigrants were strongly put forth, in various publications. The work of Roberts was the first of these, and was followed in a few years by those of Bartram, Stork, and Romans. The works of both Roberts and Stork, contain plans and minute descriptions of St. Augustine. The plan of the town in Stork, represents every building, lot, garden, and flower-bed in the place, and gives a very accurate view of its general appearance.

The descriptions vary somewhat. Roberts, who published his work the year of the cession, 1763, shows in connection with his plan of the town, an Indian village on the point south of the city, at the powder-house, and another just north of the city.

The one to the north has a church. A negro fort is shown about a mile to the northward. Oglethorpe's landing place is shown on Anastasia Island, and a small fort on the main land south of the city. The depth of water on the bar is marked as being at low water, eight feet.

Roberts describes the city as "running along the shore at the foot of a pleasant hill, adorned with trees; its form is oblong, divided by four regular streets, crossing each other at right angles; down by the sea side, about three-fourths of a mile south of the town, standeth the church, and a monastery of St. Augustine. The best built part of the town is on the north side, leading to the castle, which is called St. John's Fort. It is a square building of soft stone, fortified with whole bastions, having a rampart of twenty feet high, with a parapet nine feet high, and it is casemated. The town is fortified with bastions, and with cannon. On the north and south, without the walls of the city, are the Indian towns."

The next plan we have, is in the work by Dr. Stork, the third edition of which was published in 1769. He gives a beautiful plan of the place. Shows the fort as it now exists, with its various outworks; three churches are designated, one on the public square at its southwest corner; another on St. George street, on the lot on the west side, south of Green

Spanish Coat of Arms over the Entrance to Fort Marion.

lane, and a Dutch church near where the Roman
Catholic cemetery now exists.   From the size of the
plan, it does not embrace the Indian village.   The
present United States Court-house was the governor's official residence, and is represented as
having attached to it a beautiful garden.   The
Franciscan house or convent, is shown where the
barracks are now, but different in the form of the
buildings.   With the exception of the disappearance
of a part of one street then existing, there appears
very little change from the present plan of the town
and buildings.

He describes the fort as being finished " according
to the modern taste of military architecture," and as
making a very handsome appearance, and "that it
might justly be deemed the prettiest fort in the
king's dominion."   He omits the pleasant hill from
his description, and says " the town is situated near
the glacis of the fort ; the streets are regularly laid
out, and built narrow for the purposes of shade.   It is
above half a mile in length, regularly fortified with
bastions, half-bastions, and a ditch ; that it had also
several rows of the Spanish bayonet along the
ditch, which formed so close a chevaux de frize,
with their pointed leaves, as to be impenetrable ; the
southern bastions were built of stone.   In the
middle of the town is a spacious square, called the

parade, open towards the harbor; at the bottom of the square is the governor's house, the apartments of which are spacious and suitable; suited to the climate, with high windows, a balcony in front, and galleries on both sides; to the back of the house is joined a tower, called in America a look-out, from which there is an extensive prospect towards the sea, as well as inland. There are two churches within the walls of the town, the parish church, a plain building, and another belonging to the convent of Franciscan Friars, which is converted into barracks for the garrison. The houses are built of free-stone, commonly two stories high, two rooms upon a floor, with large windows and balconies; before the entry of most of the houses, runs a portico of stone arches. The roofs are commonly flat. The Spaniards consulted convenience more than taste in their buildings. The number of houses within the town and lines, when the Spaniards left it, was about nine hundred; many of them, especially in the suburbs, being built of wood are now gone to decay. The inhabitants were of all colors, whites, negroes, mulattoes, Indians, &c. At the evacuation of St. Augustine, the population was five thousand seven hundred, including the garrison of two thousand five hundred men. Half a mile from the town to the west, is a line with a broad ditch and bastions, running from

the St. Sebastian creek to St. Marks river.   A mile
further is another fortified line with some redoubts,
forming a second communication between a stoccata
fort upon St. Sebastian river and Fort Moosa, upon
St. Marks river.

" Within the first line near the town, was a small
settlement of Germans, who had a church of their
own.   Upon the St. Marks river, within the second
line, was also an Indian town, with a church built
of freestone ; what is very remarkable, it is in good
taste, though built by the Indians."

The two lines of defense here spoken of, may still
be traced.   The nearest one is less than one-fourth
of a mile from the city gate, and the other at the
well-known place called the stoccades, the stakes
driven to form which, still distinctly mark the place ;
and the ditch and embankment can be traced for a
considerable distance through the grounds attached
to my residence.

A letter-writer, who dates at St. Augustine, May,
1774, says " This town is now truly become a heap
of ruins, a fit receptacle for the wretches of inhabitants."   (Rather a dyspeptic description, in all probability.)

A bridge was built across the Sebastian river by
the English, " but the great depth of the water,
joined to the instability of the bottom, did not suffer

it to remain long, and a ferry is now established in its room; the keeper of the ferry has fifty pounds per annum allowed him, and the inhabitants pay nothing for crossing, except after dark."

The English constructed large buildings for barracks, characterized by Romans " as such stupendous piles of buildings, which were large enough to contain five regiments, when it is a matter of great doubt, whether there will ever be a necessity to keep one whole regiment here. The material for this great barracks was brought from New York, and far inferior to those found on the spot; yet the freight alone, amounted to more than their value when landed. It makes us almost believe," says the elaborate Romans, " that all this show is in vain, or at most, that the English were so much in dread of musquitoes, that they thought a large army requisite to drive off these formidable foes. To be serious," says he, " this fort and barracks, add not a little to the beauty of the prospect; but most men would think that the money spent on this useless parade, would have been better laid out on roads and fences through the province; or, if it must be in forts, why not at Pensacola?"

There is a manuscript work of John Gerard Williams de Bahm, existing in the library of Harvard University, which contains some particulars of interest, relative to Florida at the period of the English occupation.

He states the number of inhabitants of East Florida, which in those days meant mostly St. Augustine, from 1663 to 1771, as follows: householders, besides women, &c., two hundred and eighty-eight; imported by Mr. Trumbull from Minorca, &c., one thousand four hundred; negroes, upwards of nine hundred. Of these, white heads of families, one hundred and forty-four were married, which is just one-half; thirty-one are store-keepers and traders; three haberdashers, fifteen innkeepers, forty-five artificers and mechanics, one hundred and ten planters, four hunters, six cow-keepers, eleven overseers, twelve draftsmen in employ of government, besides mathematicians; fifty-eight had left the province; twenty-eight dead, of whom four were killed acting as constables, two hanged for pirating. Among the names of those then residing in East Florida are mentioned, Sir Charles Burdett, William Drayton, Esq., planter, Chief Justice; Rev. John Forbes, parson, Judge of Admiralty and Councillor; Rev. N. Fraser, parson at Mosquito; Governor James Grant, Hon. John Moultrie, planter and Lieutenant Governor; William Stork, Esq., historian; Andrew Turnbull, Esq., H. M. Counselor; Bernard Romans, draftsman, &c.; William Bartram, planter; James Moultrie, Esq.

He says, The light house on Anastasia Island had been constructed and built of mason-work by the Spaniards ; and, in 1769, by order of Gen. Haldimand, it was raised sixty feet higher in carpenter's work, had a cannon planted on the top, which is fired the very moment the flag is hoisted, for a signal to the town and pilots that a vessel is off. The light house has two flag-staffs, one to the south and one to the north ; on either of which the flag is hoisted, viz., to the south if the vessel comes from thence, and the north if the vessel comes that way.

" The town is situated in a healthy zone, is surrounded with salt water marshes, not at all prejudicial to health ; their evaporations are swept away in the day time by the easterly winds, and in the night season by the westerly winds trading back to the eastward. At the time when the Spaniards left the town, all the gardens were well stocked with fruit trees, viz., figs, guavas, plantain, pomegranates, lemons, limes, citrons, shadock, bergamot, China and Seville oranges, the latter full of fruit throughout the whole winter season ; and the pot-herbs, though suspended in their vegetation, were seldom destroyed by cold. The town is three-quarters of a mile in length, but not quite a quarter wide ; had four churches ornamentally built with stone in the Spanish taste, of which one within and one without

the town still exist. One is pulled down; that is
the German church, but the steeple is preserved as
an ornament to the town; and the othei, viz., the
convent church and convent in town is taken in the
body of the barracks. All houses are built of ma-
sonry; their entrances are shaded by piazzas, supported by Tuscan pillars or pilasters; against the
south sun. The houses have to the east windows
projecting sixteen or eighteen inches into the street,
very wide, and proportionally high. On the west
side, their windows are commonly very small, and
no opening of any kind to the north, on which side
they have double walls six or eight feet asunder,
forming a kind of gallery, which answers for cellars
and pantries. Before most of the entrances were
arbors of vines, producing plenty and very good
grapes. No house has any chimney for a fire-place;
the Spaniards made use of stone urns, filled them
with coals left in their kitchens in the afternoon,
and set them at sunset in their bed-rooms, to defend
themselves against those winter seasons, which
required such care. The governor's residence has
both sides piazzas, viz., a double one to the south,
and a single one to the north; also a Belvidere and
a grand portico decorated with Doric pillars and
entablatures. On the north end of the town is a
casemated fort, with four bastions, a ravelin, counter-

scarp, and a glacis built with quarried shell-stones, and constructed according to the rudiments of Marechal de Vauban. This fort commands the road of the bay, the town, its environs, and both Tolomako stream and Matanzas creek. The soil in the gardens and environs of the town is chiefly sandy and marshy. The Spaniards seem to have had a notion of manuring their land with shells one foot deep.

" Among the three thousand who evacuated St. Augustine, the author is credibly informed, were many Spaniards near and above the age of one hundred years, (observe) this nation, especially natives of St. Augustine, bore the reputation of great sobriety." *

On the 3d of January, 1766, the thermometer sunk to 26°, with the wind from N. W. " The ground was frozen an inch thick on the banks; this was the fatal night that destroyed the lime, citron, and banana trees in St. Augustine, many curious evergreens up the river that were twenty years old in a flourishing state." † In 1774, there was a snow storm, which extended over most of the province. The ancient inhabitants still (1836) speak of it as an extraordinary white rain. It was said to have done little damage.‡

---

* De Brahm MS., p. 192. † Stork, p. 11.
‡ Williams' Florida., p 17.

In this connection, and as it is sometimes supposed that the climate is now colder than formerly,
it may be stated that the thermometer went very
low in 1799. East Florida suffered from a violent
frost on the 6th April, 1828. In February, 1835,
the thermometer sunk to 7° above zero, wind from
N. W.; and the St. Johns river was frozen several
rods from the shore; all kinds of fruit trees were
killed to the ground, and the wild orange trees suffered as well as the cultivated.

Dr. Nicolas Turnbull, in the year 1767, associated
with Sir William Duncan and other Englishmen
of note, projected a colony of European emigrants to
be settled at New Smyrna. He brought from the
islands of Greece, Corsica, and Minorca, some fourteen hundred persons, agreeing to convey them free
of expense, find them in clothing and provisions,
and, at the end of three years, to give fifty acres of
land to each head of a family, and twenty-five to
each child. After a long passage they arrived out,
and formed the settlement. The principal article of
cultivation produced by them was indigo, which
commanded a high price, and was assisted by a
bounty from the English government. After a few
years, Turnbull, as is alleged, either from avarice or
natural cruelty, assumed a control the most absolute

12

over these colonists, and practiced cruelties the most painful upon them.

An insurrection took place in 1769 among them, in consequence of severe punishments; which was speedily repressed, and the leaders of it brought to trial before the English court at St. Augustine ; five of the number were convicted and sentenced to death. Gov. Grant pardoned two of the five, and a third was released upon the condition of his becoming the executioner of the other two. Nine years after the commencement of their settlement, their number had become reduced from 1,400 to 600. In 1776, proceedings were instituted on their behalf by Mr. Yonge, the attorney-general of the province, which resulted in their being exonerated from their contract with Turnbull; lands were thereupon assigned them in the northern part of the city, which was principally built up by them ; and their descendants, at the present day, form the larger portion of the population of the place.

Governor Grant was the first English governor, and was a gentleman of much energy ; and during his term of office, he projected many great and permanent improvements in the province. The public roads, known as the king's roads, from St. Augustine to New Smyrna, and from St. Augustine to Jacksonville, and thence to Coleraine, were then constructed, and remain a lasting monument of his wisdom and desire of improvement.

Gov. Tonyn succeeded Gov. Grant; and a legislative council was authorized to assemble, and the pretense and forms of a constitutional government were gone through with.

In August, 1775, a British vessel, called the Betsey, Capt. Lofthouse, from London, with 111 barrels of powder, was captured off the bar of St. Augustine, by an American privateer from Charleston, very much to the disgust and annoyance of the British authorities.

At this period, St. Augustine assumed much importance as a depot and *point d'appui* for the British forces in their operations against the Southern States; and very considerable forces were at times assembled.

In the excess of the zeal and loyalty of the garrison and inhabitants of St. Augustine, upon the receipt of the news of the American Declaration of Independence, the effigies of John Hancock and Samuel Adams were burned upon the public square, where the monument now stands.

The expedition of Gen. Prevost against Savannah was organized and embarked from St. Augustine, in 1779.

Sixty of the most distinguished citizens of Carolina

were seized by the British in 1780, and transported to St. Augustine as prisoners of war and hostages, among whom were Arthur Middleton, Edward Rutledge, Gen. Gadsden, and Mr. Calhoun; all were put upon parol except Gen. Gadsden and Mr. Calhoun, who refused the indulgence, and were committed to the fort, where they remained many months close prisoners. Gen. Rutherford and Col. Isaacs, of North Carolina, were also transported hither, and committed to the fort.

An expedition was fitted out from St. Augustine in 1783, to act against New Providence, under Col. Devereux; and, with very slender means, that able officer succeeded in capturing and reducing the Bahamas, which have ever since remained under English domination.

The expense of supporting the government of East Florida during the English occupation, was very considerable, amounting to the sum of £122,000. The exports of Florida, in 1778, amounted to £48,000; and, in 1772, the province exported 40,000 lbs. indigo; and in 1782, 20,000 barrels of turpentine.

CHAPTER XVI.

RE-CESSION OF FLORIDA TO SPAIN—ERECTION OF THE PARISH
CHURCH—CHANGE OF FLAGS.—1783—1821.

In June, 1784, in fulfillment of the treaty between England and Spain, Florida, after twenty
years of British occupation, was re-ceded to the
Spanish crown, and taken possession of by Governor
Zespedez.

The English residents, in general, left* the country, and went either to the Bahamas, Jamaica, or the
United States. Those who went to the British islands were almost ruined; but those who settled in
the States were more successful.

In April, 1793, the present Roman Catholic church
was commenced, the previous church having been in
another portion of the city.† It was constructed

---

* Among the families remaining were the Fatios, Flemings, and a few
others.

† The old parish church was on St. George street, on west side of the
street.

under the direction of Don Mariana de la Rocque
and Don P. Berrio, government engineer-officers.
The cost of the church was $16,650, of which about
$6,000 was received from the proceeds of the mate-
rials and ornaments of the old churches, about
$1,000 from the contributions of the inhabitants,
and the remaining $10,000 furnished by the govern-
ment. One of its four bells has the following inscription, showing it to be probably the oldest bell in this
country, being now 175 years old.

Sancte Joseph
Ora Pro Nobis
D 1682

Don Enrique White was for many years governor
of Florida, and died in the city of St. Augustine.
He is spoken of, by those who knew him, in high
terms, for his integrity and openness of character;
and many amusing anecdotes are related connected
with his eccentricities.

In 1812, the American government, being appre-
hensive that Great Britain designed obtaining possession of Florida, sent its troops into the province,
overrunning and destroying the whole country. The
manner and the pretenses under which this was done,

reflect but little credit on the United States government; and the transparent sham of taking possession of the country by the patriots, supported by United States troops, was as undignified as it was futile. It is for the damages occasioned by this invasion, that the " Florida claims " for "losses" of its citizens have been presented to the government of the United States. The *principal* of the damages sustained, that is to say, the actual value of the property then destroyed, has been allowed and paid; but the interest, or damages for the detention, has been withheld upon the ground that the government does not pay interest. The treaty between the United States and Spain in reference to the cession of Florida to the United States, requires the United States to make *satisfaction* for such claims; and the payment of the bare amount of actual loss, after a detention of thirty years, is considered by the claimants an inadequate *satisfaction* of a just claim.

In the spring of 1818, General Jackson made his celebrated incursion into Florida, and by a series of energetic movements followed the Seminoles and Creeks to their fastnesses, and forever crushed the power of those formidable tribes for offensive operations.

In the latter part of 1817, a revolutionary party took possession of Amelia Island, and raised a *soi disant patriot* flag at Fernandina, supported mainly in the enterprise by adventurers from the United States: M'Gregor was assisted by officers of the United States army. An expedition was sent from St. Augustine by the Spanish governor to eject the invaders, which failed. One Aury, an English adventurer, for a time held command there; and also a Mr. Hubbard, formerly sheriff of New York, who was the civil governor, and died there. The United States troops eventually interfered; but negotiations for the cession put a stop to further hostilities.

The king of Spain, finding his possessions in Florida utterly worthless to his crown, and only an expense to sustain the garrisons, while the repeated attempts to disturb its political relations prevented any beneficial progress towards its settlement, gladly agreed, in 1819, to a transfer of Florida to the United States for five millions of dollars.

An English gentleman who visited St. Augustine in 1817, gives his impressions of the place as follows: " Emerging from the solitudes and shades of the pine forests, we espied the distant yet distinct lights of the watch towers of the fortress of St. Augustine, delightful beacons to my weary pilgrimage. The clock was striking ten as I reached the foot of the drawbridge; the sentinels were passing the *alerto*, as I demanded entrance; having answered the prelimi-

nary questions, the draw-bridge was slowly lowered.
The officer of the guard, having received my name
and wishes, sent a communication to the governor,
who issued orders for my immediate admission. On
opening the gate, the guard was ready to receive
me; and a file of men, with their officer, escorted me
to his Excellency, who expressed his satisfaction at
my revisit to Florida. I soon retired to the luxury
of repose, and the following morning was greeted as
an old acquaintance by the members of this little
community.

"I had arrived at a season of general relaxation,
on the eve of the carnival, which is celebrated with
much gayety in all Catholic countries. Masks, domi-
noes, harlequins, punchinellos, and a great variety of
grotesque disguises, on horseback, in cars, gigs, and on
foot, paraded the streets with guitars, violins, and
other instruments; and in the evenings, the houses
were open to receive masks, and balls were given in
every direction. I was told that in their better days,
when their pay was regularly remitted from the Ha-
vanna, these amusements were admirably conducted,
and the rich dresses exhibited on these occasions,
were not eclipsed by their more fashionable friends
in Cuba; but poverty had lessened their spirit for
enjoyment, as well as the means for procuring it;
enough, however remained to amuse an idle specta-

tor, and I entered with alacrity into their diversions.

"About thirty of the hunting warriors of the Seminoles, with their squaws, had arrived, for the purpose of selling the produce of the chase, consisting of bear, deer, tiger, and other skins, bears' grease, and other trifling articles. This savage race, once the lords of the ascendant, are the most formidable border enemies of the United States. This party had arrived, after a range of six months, for the purposes of sale and barter. After trafficking for their commodities, they were seen at various parts of the town, assembled in small groups, seated upon their haunches, like monkeys, passing round their bottles of *aqua dente* (the rum of Cuba), their repeated draughts upon which soon exhausted their contents; they then slept off the effects of intoxication under the walls, exposed to the influence of the sun. Their appearance was extremely wretched ; their skins of a dark, dirty, chocolate color, with long, straight, black hair, over which they had spread a quantity of bears' grease. In their ears, and the cartilages of the nose, were inserted rings of silver and brass, with pendants of various shapes; their features prominent and harsh, and their eyes had a wild and ferocious expression.

" A torn blanket, or an ill-fashioned dirty linen

jacket, is the general costume of these Indians; a triangular piece of cloth passes around the loins; the women vary in their apparel by merely wearing short petticoats, the original colors of which were not distinguishable from the various incrustations of dirt. Some of the young squaws were tolerably agreeable, and if well washed and dressed would not have been uninteresting; but the elder squaws wore the air of misery and debasement.

"The garrison is composed of a detachment from the Royal regiment of Cuba, with some *black* troops; who together form a respectable force. The fort and bastions are built of the same material as the houses of the town, *coquina*. This marine substance is superior to stone, not being liable to splinter from the effects of bombardment; it receives and embeds the shot, which adds rather than detracts from its strength and security.

"The houses and the rear of the town are intersected and covered with orange groves; their golden fruit and deep green foliage, not only render the air agreeable, but beautify the appearance of this interesting little town, in the centre of which (the square) rises a large structure dedicated to the Catholic religion. At the upper end are the remains of a very considerable house, the former residence of the governor of this settlement; but now (1817), in a

state of dilapidation and decay, from age and inat-
tention.

"At the southern extremity of the town stands a
large building, formerly a monastery of Carthusian
Friars, but now occupied as a barrack for the troops
of the garrison. At a little distance are four stacks
of chimnies, the sole remains of a beautiful range of
barracks, built during the occupancy of the British
from 1763 to 1783; for three years the 29th regiment was stationed there, and in that time they did
not lose a single man. The proverbial salubrity of
the climate, has obtained for St. Augustine the designation of the Montpelier of North America; indeed,
such is the general character of the Province of East
Florida.

"The governor (Coppinger), is about forty-five
years of age, of active and vigorous mind, anxious
to promote by every means in his power the prosperity of the province confided to his command; his
urbanity and other amiable qualities render him
accessible to the meanest individual, and justice is
sure to follow an appeal to his decision. His military talents are well known, and appreciated by his
sovereign; and he now holds, in addition to the
government of East Florida, the rank of Colonel in
the Royal Regiment of Cuba.

"The clergy consist of the *padre* (priest of the

parish), Father Cosby, a native of Wexford, in
Ireland; a Franciscan friar, the chaplain to the garrison, and an inferior or curé.   The social qualities of
the *padre*, and the general tolerance of his feelings,
render him an acceptable visitor to all his flock.
The judge, treasurer, collector, and notary, are the
principal officers of the establishment, besides a
number of those devoted solely to the military occu-
pations of the garrison.   The whole of this society
is extremely courteous to strangers;   they form one
family, and those little jealousies and animosities, so
disgraceful to our small English communities, do not
sully their meetings of friendly chit-chat, called as
in Spain, *turtulias*.   The women are deservedly
celebrated for their charms; their lovely black eyes
have a vast deal of expression; their complexions
a clear brunette; much attention is paid to the
arrangement of their hair; at mass they are always
well dressed in black silk *basquinas* (petticoats),
with the little *mantilla* (black lace veil) over their
heads; the men in their military costumes; good
order and temperance are their characteristic virtues;
but the vice of gambling too often profanes their
social haunts, from which even the fair sex are not
excluded.   Two days following our arrival, a ball
was given by some of the inhabitants, to which I
was invited.   The elder couples opened it with

minuets, succeeded by the younger couples display-
ing their handsome light figures in Spanish dances."*

The old inhabitants still speak in terms of fond
regret of the beauty of the place when embowered
in its orange groves, and the pleasantness of its old
customs and usages. Dancing formed one of their
most common amusements, as it now does. The
posey dance, now become obsolete, was then of
almost daily occurrence, and was introduced in the
following manner. The females of the family erect
in a room of their house, a neat little arbor dressed
with pots and garlands of flowers, and lit up brightly
with candles. This is understood by the gentlemen
as an invitation to drop in and admire the beauty of
their decorations. In the mean time, the lady who
has prepared it, selects a partner from among her
visitors, and in token of her preference honors him
with a bouquet of flowers. The gentleman who
receives the bouquet becomes then, for the nonce,
king of the ball, and leads out the fair donor as
queen of the dance; the others take partners, and
the ball is thus inaugurated, and may continue several successive evenings. Should the lady's choice
fall upon an unwilling swain, which seldom happened, he could be excused by assuming the expenses

---

* Voyage to Spanish Main. London, 1819. Page 116, *et seq.*

of the entertainment. These assemblies were always informal, and frequented by all classes, all meeting on a level; but were conducted with the utmost politeness and decorum, for which the Spanish character is so distinguished.

The carnival amusements are still kept up to some extent, but with little of the taste and wit which formerly characterized them, and without which they degenerate into mere buffoonery.

The graceful Spanish dance, so well suited in its slow and regular movements to the inhabitants of a warm climate, has always retained the preference with the natives of the place, who dance it with that native grace and elegance of movement which seems easy and natural for every one, but is seldom equaled by the Anglo-Saxon.

CHAPTER XVII.

TRANSFER OF FLORIDA TO THE UNITED STATES—AMERICAN OCCUPATION—ANCIENT BUILDINGS, ETC.

On the 10th day of July, in the year 1821, the standard of Spain, which had been raised two hundred and fifty-six years before, over St. Augustine, was finally lowered forever from the walls over which it had so long fluttered, and the stars and stripes of the youngest of nations, rose where sooner or later the hand of destiny would assuredly have placed them.

It was intended that the change of flags should have taken place on the 4th of July; owing to a detention, this was frustrated; but the inhabitants celebrated the 4th with a handsome public ball at the governor's house.

The Spanish garrison, and officers connected with it, returned to Cuba, and some of the Spanish families; but the larger portion of the inhabitants remained. A considerable influx of inhabitants from the adjoining States took place, and the town speedily assumed a somewhat American character. The proportion of American population since the change of flags, has been about one third. Most of the native inhabitants converse with equal fluency in either language.

In the year 1823, the legislative council of Florida held its second session in the government house at St. Augustine. Governor W. P. Duval was the first governor after the organization of the territory. The Ralph Ringwood Sketches of Irving have given a wide celebrity to the character of our worthy and original first governor, now recently deceased.

During the month of February, 1835, East Florida was visited by a frost much more severe than any before experienced. A severe northwest wind blew ten days in succession, but more violently for about three days. During this period, the mercury sunk to seven degrees above zero. The St. Johns river was frozen several rods from the shore. All kinds of fruit trees were killed to the ground; many of them never started again, even from the roots. The wild groves suffered equally with those cultivated. The orange had become the staple of Florida commerce; several millions were exported from the St. Johns and St. Augustine during the two previous years. Numerous groves had just been planted out, and extensive nurseries could hardly supply the demand for young trees. Some of the groves had, during the previous autumn, brought to their owners, one, two, and three thousand dollars; and the

13

increasing demand for this fruit, opened in prospect mines of wealth to the inhabitants.

"Then came a frost, a withering frost."

Some of the orange groves in East Florida were estimated at from five to ten thousand dollars, and even more. They were at once rendered valueless. The larger part of the population at St. Augustine had been accustomed to depend on the produce of their little groves of eight or ten trees, to purchase their coffee, sugar, and other necessaries from the stores; they were left without resource.

"The town of St. Augustine, that heretofore appeared like a rustic village, their white houses peeping from among the clustered boughs and golden fruit of their favorite tree, beneath whose shade the foreign invalid cooled his fevered limbs, and imbibed health from the fragrant air,—how was she fallen! Dry, unsightly poles, with ragged bark, stick up around her dwellings; and where the mocking-bird once delighted to build her nest, and tune her lovely songs, owls hoot at night, and sterile winds whistle through the leafless branches. Never was a place rendered more desolate."*

The groves were at once re-planted, and soon bid fair to yield most abundantly; when, in 1842, an insect was introduced into the country, called the *orange coccus*, which spread over the whole country

---

* Williams' Florida, pp. 18, *et seq.*

with wonderful rapidity, and almost totally destroyed every tree it fastened upon. Of late, the ravages of this insect seem less destructive, and the groves have begun to resume their bearing; these add to the beauty of the residences at St. Augustine, with their glossy, deep-green leaves, and golden fruit; and hopes of an entire restoration are now confidently entertained.

In December, 1835, the war with the Seminole Indians broke out; and for some years St. Augustine was full of the pomp and circumstance of war. It was dangerous to venture beyond the gates; and many sad scenes of Indian massacre took place in the neighborhood of the city. During this period, great apparent prosperity prevailed; property was valuable, rents were high; speculators projected one city on the north of the town, and another on the west; a canal to the St. Johns, and also a railroad to Picolata; and great hopes of future prosperity were entertained. With the cessation of the war, the importance of St. Augustine diminished; younger communities took the lead of it, aided by superior advantages of location, and greater enterprise, and St. Augustine has subsided into the pleasant, quiet, *dolce far niente* of to-day, living upon its old memories, contented, peaceful, and agreeable, and likely to remain without much change for the future.

Of the public buildings, it may be remarked that the extensive British barracks were destroyed by fire in 1792; and that the Franciscan Convent was occupied as it had been before, as barracks for the troops not in garrison in the fort. The appearance of these buildings has been much changed, by the extensive repairs and alterations made by the United States government. It had formerly a large circular look-out upon the top, from which a beautiful view of the surrounding country was obtained. Its walls are probably the oldest foundations in the city.

The present United States Court-house, now occupied by many public offices, was the residence of the Spanish governors. It has been rebuilt by the United States; and its former quaint and interesting appearance has been lost, in removing its look-out tower, and balconies, and the handsome gateway, mentioned by De Brahm, which is said to have been a fine specimen of Doric architecture.*

Trinity Episcopal Church was commenced in 1827, and consecrated in 1833, by Bishop Bowen, of South Carolina. The Presbyterian Church was built about 1830, and the Methodist chapel about 1846.

The venerable-looking building on the bay, at the corner of Green lane and Bay street, is considered the oldest building in the place, and has evidently,

---

* It is said to have been taken down by the contractor, to form the foundation of his kitchen.

been a fine building in its day.   It was the residence
of the attorney-general, in English times.

The monument on the public square was erected
in 1812-13, upon the information of the adoption of
the Spanish constitution, as a memorial of that event,
in pursuance of a royal order to that effect, directed
to the public authorities of all the provincial towns.
Geronimo Alvarez was the Alcalde under whose
direction it was erected.   The plan of it was made
by Sr. Hernandez, the father of the late General
Hernandez.   A short time after it was put up, the
Spanish constitution having had a downfall, orders
were issued by the government, that all the mon-
uments erected to the constitution throughout its
dominions, should be demolished.   The citizens of
St. Augustine were unwilling to see their monument
torn down; and, with the passive acquiescence of the
governor, the marble tablets inscribed PLAZA DE LA
CONSTITUCION being removed, the monument itself
was allowed to stand; and it thus remains to this
day, the only monument in existence to commemorate the farce of the constitution of 1812.   In 1818,
the tablets were restored without objection.

The bridge and causeway are the work of the
government of the United States.   The present
sea-wall was built between 1835 and 1842, by the
United States, at an expense of one hundred thousand dollars.

CHAPTER XVIII.

PRESENT APPEARANCE OF ST. AUGUSTINE, AS GIVEN BY THE
AUTHOR OF THANOTOPSIS—ITS CLIMATE AND SALUBRITY.

St. Augustine has now attained, for this side of
the Atlantic, a period of most respectable antiquity.
In a country like America, where States are ushered
into existence in the full development of maturity,
where large cities rise like magic from the rude
forest, where the "oldest inhabitant" recollects the
cutting down of the lofty elms which shadowed the
wigwam of the red man, perchance on some spot
now in the heart of a great city; an antiquity of
three centuries would be esteemed as almost reaching back (compared with modern growth) to the
days of the Pharaohs.

The larger number of the early settlements were
unsuitably located, and were forced to be abandoned
on account of their unhealthiness; but the Spanish
settlement at St. Augustine has remained for near
three hundred years where it was originally planted;
and the health of its inhabitants has, for this long
period, given it a deserved reputation for salubrity,
and exemption from disease, attributable to locality
or extraneous influences or causes.

The great age attained by its inhabitants was

CITY GATES, St AUGUSTINE.

remarked by De Brahm; the number and health-
fulness of the children that throng its streets, attract
now, as they did then, the attention of strangers.
This salubrity is easily accounted for, by the almost
insular position of the city, upon a narrow neck of
land nearly surrounded by salt water; the main
shore, a high and healthy pine forest and sandy
plains, so near the ocean as to be fanned by its
constant breezes, and within the sound of its echoing
waves; a situation combining more local advantages
for salubrity could hardly be imagined. While it
will never probably increase to any great extent in
population, it will hardly be likely to decrease. Its
health, easy means of support, unambitious class of
inhabitants, with their strong attachments, and family and local ties, will contribute to maintain St.
Augustine as the time-honored ancient city, with its
permanent population, and its visitors for health, for
centuries perhaps yet to come.

I cannot perhaps better conclude these historic
notices than by giving the impressions of the author
of Thanatopsis,* one whose poetic fame will endure
as long as American literature exists. Writing from
St. Augustine in April, 1843, he says,—

"At length we emerged upon a shrubby plain,
and finally came in sight of this oldest city of the

---

* Bryant.

United States, seated among its trees on a sandy swell of land, where it has stood for three hundred years. I was struck with its ancient and homely aspect, even at a distance, and could not help likening it to pictures which I had seen of Dutch towns, though it wanted a wind-mill or two to make the resemblance perfect. We drove into a green square, in the midst of which was a monument erected to commemorate the Spanish constitution of 1812, and thence through the narrow streets of the city to our hotel.

"I have called the streets narrow. In few places are they wide enough to allow two carriages to pass abreast. I was told that they were not originally intended for carriages; and that in the time when the town belonged to Spain, many of them were floored with an artificial stone, composed of shells and mortar, which in this climate takes and keeps the hardness of rock; and that no other vehicle than a hand-barrow was allowed to pass over them. In some places you see remnants of this ancient pavement; but for the most part it has been ground into dust under the wheels of the carts and carriages introduced by the new inhabitants. The old houses, built of a kind of stone which is seemingly a pure concretion of small shells, overhang the streets with their wooden balconies; and the gardens between the houses are fenced on the side of the street with

high walls of stone. Peeping over these walls you
see branches of the pomegranate, and of the orange-
tree now fragrant with flowers, and, rising yet higher,
the leaning boughs of the fig with its broad luxuriant
leaves. Occasionally you pass the ruins of houses—
walls of stone with arches and stair-cases of the same
material, which once belonged to stately dwellings.
You meet in the streets with men of swarthy complexions and foreign physiognomy, and you hear
them speaking to each other in a strange language.
You are told that these are the remains of those who
inhabited the country under the Spanish dominion,
and that the dialect you have heard is that of the
island of Minorca.

" 'Twelve years ago,' said an acquaintance of mine,
' when I first visited St. Augustine, it was a fine old
Spanish town. A large proportion of the houses
which you now see roofed like barns, were then flat-
roofed; they were all of shell rock, and these modern wooden buildings were then not erected. That
old fort which they are now repairing, to fit it for
receiving a garrison, was a sort of ruin, for the outworks had partly fallen, and it stood unoccupied by
the military, a venerable monument of the Spanish
dominion. But the orange-groves were the wealth
and ornament of St. Augustine, and their produce
maintained the inhabitants in comfort. Orange-trees
of the size and height of the pear-tree, often rising

higher than the roofs of the houses, embowered the
town in perpetual verdure. They stood so close in
the groves that they excluded the sun; and the
atmosphere was at all times aromatic with their
leaves and fruit, and in spring the fragrance of the
flowers was almost oppressive.'

"The old fort of St. Mark, now called Fort Marion,
—a foolish change of name—is a noble work, frowning
over the Matanzas, which flows between St. Augustine and the island of Anastasia; and it is worth
making a long journey to see. No record remains
of its original construction; but it is supposed to
have been erected about a hundred and fifty years
since,* and the shell rock of which it is built is dark
with time. We saw where it had been struck with
cannon balls, which, instead of splitting the rock,
became imbedded and clogged among the loosened
fragments of shell. This rock is therefore one of the
best materials for fortification in the world. We
were taken into the ancient prisons of the fort-dun-
geons, one of which was dimly lighted by a grated
window, and another entirely without light; and by
the flame of a torch we were shown the half obliter-
ated inscriptions scrawled on the walls long ago by
prisoners. But in another corner of the fort, we
were taken to look at the secret cells, which were

---

* It is much more ancient.

discovered a few years since in consequence of the
sinking of the earth over a narrow apartment between them. These cells are deep under ground,
vaulted over-head, and without windows. In one of
them a wooden machine was found, which some supposed might have been a rack, and in the other a
quantity of human bones. The doors of these cells
had been walled up and concealed with stucco, before
the fort passed into the hands of the Americans.

"You cannot be in St. Augustine a day without
hearing some of its inhabitants speak of its agreeable
climate. During the sixteen days of my residence
here, the weather has certainly been as delightful as
I could imagine. We have the temperature of early
June as June is known in New York. The morn-
ings are sometimes a little sultry; but after two or
three hours a fresh breeze comes in from the sea
sweeping through the broad piazzas, and breathing
in at the windows. At this season it comes laden
with the fragrance of the flowers of the Pride of
India, and sometimes of the orange tree, and sometimes brings the scent of roses, now in bloom. The
nights are gratefully cool; and I have been told by
a person who has lived here many years, that there
are very few nights in summer when you can sleep
without a blanket.

"An acquaintance of mine, an invalid, who has
tried various climates, and has kept up a kind of

running fight with death for many years, retreating from country to country as he pursued, declares to me that the winter climate of St. Augustine is to be preferred to that of any part of Europe, even that of Sicily, and that it is better than the climate of the West Indies. He finds it genial and equable, at the same time that it is not enfeebling. The summer heats are prevented from being intense by the sea-breeze, of which I have spoken. I have looked over the work of Dr. Forry on the climate of the United States, and have been surprised to see the uniformity of climate which he ascribes to Key West. As appears by the observations he has collected, the seasons at that place glide into each other by the softest gradations; and the heat never, even in midsummer, reaches that extreme which is felt in the higher latitudes of the American continent. The climate of Florida is, in fact, an insular climate: the Atlantic on the east, and the Gulf of Mexico on the west, temper the airs that blow over it, making them cooler in summer and warmer in winter. I do not wonder, therefore, that it is so much the resort of invalids; it would be more so if the softness of its atmosphere, and the beauty and serenity of its seasons were generally known. Nor should it be supposed that accommodations for persons in delicate health are wanting; they are, in fact, becoming better with every year as the demand for them increases. Among the acquaintances whom I have made here, I remember many who having come hither for the benefit of their health, are detained for life by the amenity of the climate. 'It seems to me,' said an intelligent gentleman of this class, the other day, 'as if I could not exist out of Florida. When I go to the north, I feel most sensibly the severe extremes of the weather; the climate of Charleston itself appears harsh to me.'

"The negroes of St. Augustine are a good-looking specimen of the race, and have the appearance of being very well treated. You rarely see a negro in ragged clothing; and the colored children, though slaves, are often dressed with great neatness. In the colored people whom I saw in the Catholic church, I remarked a more agreeable, open, and gentle physiognomy than I have been accustomed to see in that class. The Spanish race blends more kindly with the African than does the English, and produces handsomer men and women.

"Some old customs which the Minorcans brought with them from their native country, are still kept up. On the evening before Easter Sunday, about eleven o'clock, I heard the sound of a serenade in the streets. Going out, I found a party of young men with instruments of music, grouped about the window of one of the dwellings, singing a hymn in honor of the Virgin,* in the Mahonese dialect. They be-

---

* This song is usually called the *Fromajardis.*

gan, as I was told, with tapping on the shutter. An answering knock within had told them that their visit was welcome, and they immediately began the serenade. If no reply had been heard, they would have passed on to another dwelling. I give the hymn as it was kindly taken down for me in writing, by a native of St. Augustine. I presume this is the first time that it has been put in print; but I fear the copy has several corruptions, occasioned by the unskillfulness of the copyist. The letter *e* which I have put in italics, represents the guttural French *e*, or, perhaps, more nearly the sound of the *u* in the word but. The *sh* of our language is represented by *sc* followed by an *i* or an *e ;* the *g*, both hard and soft, has the same sound as in our language.

> " ' Disciar*e*m lu dol
> Cantar*e*m aub' alagria
> Y n'arem a dá
> Las pascuas a Maria
> O Maria !
> " ' Sant Grabiel,
> Qui portaba la ambasciado
> Des nostro rey del cel,
> Estaran vos preñada
> Ya omitiada
> Tu o vais aqui serventa
> Fia del Dieu contenta
> Para fe lo que el vol
> Disciar*e*m lu dol, &c.
> " ' Y a milla nit
> Pariguero vos regina
> A un Dieu infinit,
> Dintra una establina.
> Y a milla dia,
> Que los angles von cantant
> Pau y abondant
> De la gloria de Dieu sol
> Disciar*e*m lu dol, &c.

" ' Y a Libalam,
Alla la terra santa
Nus nat Jesus
Aub' alagria tanta
Infant petit
Que tot lu mon salvaria
Y ningu y bastaria
Nu mes un Dieu tot sul
          Disciarem lu do!, &c.
" ' Cuant de Orion lus
Tres reys la stralla veran
Dieu omnipotent
Adora lo vingaran
Un present inferan
De mil encens y or
A lu beneit seño
Que conesce cual se vol
          Disciarem lu dol, &c.
" ' Tot fu gayant
Para cumplé la prumas
Y lu Esperit sant
De un angel fau gramas
Gran foc ences,
Que crama lu curagia
Dieu nos da lenguagia
Para fe lo que Dieu vol
          Disciarem lu dol, &c.
" ' Cuant trespasá
De quest mon nostra Señora
Al cel s' empugia
Sun fil la matescia ora
O ! Emperadora
Que del cel san eligida
Lu rosa florida
Mé resplenden que un sol
          Disciarem lu dol, &c.
" ' Y el tercer giorn
Que Jesus resunta
Dieu y Aboroma
Que la mort triumfa
De alli se ballá
Para perldra Lucife
An tot a sen pendá
Que de nostro ser el sol
          Disciarem lu dol, &c.'

"After this hymn, the following stanzas, soliciting
the customary gift of cakes or eggs, are sung:—

          " ' Ce set que vam cantant,
          Regina celestial !

Damos pan y alagria
Y bonas festas tingan
Y vos da sus bonas festas
Danos dinés de sus nous
Sempre tarem lus neans Uestas
Para recibi un grapat de nes,
Y el giorn de pascua florida
Alagramos y giuntament
As qui es mort par dar nos vida
Y via glorosiamente,
A questa casa está empedrada
Bien halla que la empedro ;
San amo de aquesta casa
Baldria duná un do
Formagiada o empanada
Cucutta a fláo ;
Cual se val casa rue grada,
Sol que no rue digas que no.'

"The shutters are then opened by the people within, and a supply of cheese, cakes or other pastry, or eggs, is dropped into a bag carried by one of the party; who acknowledge the gift in the following lines, and then depart :—

" ' Aquesta casa reta empedrada
Empedrada de cuatro vens ;
Sun amo de aquesta casa
Es omo de compliment.'

" If nothing is given, the last line reads thus :—

" 'No es homo de compliment.' "

FINIS.

INDICES.

INDEX TO *History and Antiquities.*

Jamaica, 123, 133, 135, 173
Jamestown, 122
Jesuits (Society of Jesus), 17

Keys (of Florida), 98
Key West, Florida, 196

Laudonnière, René Goulaine de, 16, 19, 20–55 passim
Lebreau, M., 40
London, England, 171
López de Mendoza Frajales, Francisco, 18, 19, 61–62, 103
"Lutherans." *See* Huguenots
Lyons, France, 34

Macarasi (Macariz), 125
Macarisqui, 125
M'Gregor, Gregor, 176
McIntosh, John, Captain, 147
Maillard, Captain, 46, 48
Manon, Francis, Father, 114
Maria Sanchez Creek, 113
Marquez Cabrera, Juan de, 124
Martínez, Pedro, Father, 100
Martyr, Peter, 13
Matanzas River, 65, 76, 168, 194
Maya, Diego de, 32, 34, 87
Mayport, Florida, 61, 103
May, River (St. Johns River), 16, 18, 24, 52–59
Menéndez de Avilés, Pedro, 17, 18, 20–110 passim
Menéndez, Juan, 94
Menéndez Marqués, Pedro, 114
Mexico, 20, 63, 98, 124, 145, 157
Mexico, Gulf of, 138, 144
Middleton, Arthur, 172
Minorca, 165, 169, 193
Minorcans, 197–200
Moore, James, Governor, 131–40
Moosa (Mosa), Fort, 144, 147, 149
Monteano (Montiano), Manuel de, 142–51, 157
Mosquito, 150
Mosquito Inlet, 64n, 76
Moultrie, James, 165

INDEX TO THE INTRODUCTION.